MOVING FROM
WHERE YOU ARE
TO THE LIFE
YOU WANT

Published by HeartSpring Media

ISBN: 978-1-58695-007-1 (hard cover)
ISBN: 978-1-58695-010-1 (soft cover)
ISBN: 978-1-58695-013-2 (ebook)

Library of Congress Control Number: 2018907600

PRINTED IN THE UNITED STATES OF AMERICA

First Printing

shift

MOVING FROM
WHERE YOU ARE
TO THE LIFE
YOU WANT

JOHN**HINKLE** RUSSELL**LAKE**

dedication

To Karen for your unwavering support of all my adventures and my parents for their continual encouragement. - Russell

To Dawn. Its been a long 24 hours. Thank you for your love and patience. To Travis, Preston, and Sam. I am most proud to be your pop.- John

The secret of change is to focus all of your energy, not on fighting the old, but on building the new.

–Socrates

table of contents

shift

It's not only moving that creates new starting points. Sometimes, all it takes is a subtle shift in perspective, an opening of the mind, an intentional pause and reset, or a new route to start to see new options and new possibilities.

\- Kristin Armstrong

chapter one

It was one of those moments you see in the movies.

You know the ones I'm talking about—the ones that give you the backstory about some poor guy who spent the better part of his career answering to a domineering and overbearing boss until one day when the boss finally gets his comeuppance, and the tables are turned; that full-circle moment when *the old boss is the one* pitching *his product* to the guy he once ridiculed for wanting to cater to his clients' whims too much with "all that touchy-feely relationship crap;" and the moment when the long-suffering guy has reinvented himself, started his own company *on his terms,* and is presented with the opportunity to return the favor of complete and total rejection of the old boss in front of his executive leadership team. Either that or choose to take the considerably less dramatic, though highly more honorable, high road and allow the moment to pass.

shift

That moment.
That set-up.
That guy.
Except the setting was no Hollywood sound stage—not even close.
It is my life.
And, I am *that guy.*

My name is David Jericho, founder and president of Jericho Enterprises, a company I am honored to lead. We were recently named as one of the global leaders in the representation and distribution industry. I've been in this business all my life, though only the last six years as head of my company. I spent nearly two-and-a-half decades right out of college working for other companies, learning the business, the products, and standard practices. I also learned a lot of *what not to do* in all those years, too.

Looking back, I can't honestly begrudge my many years spent 'paying my dues' because age has brought with it the perspective of looking back on them now and realizing those years and experiences are responsible for where I am today. Sure, I'd like to have learned the power of 'smooth transitions' in my life earlier on, but who knows, without all those lessons, I might never have arrived at what I now know to be 'the sweet spot' of life. At 52, I am fortunate enough to spend my days investing in others, working to help them find clarity and purpose, while I also work to craft a legacy of my own of intentional influence. I have discovered how to live with purpose, clarity, and focus, and the journey is amazing.

That's not to say this road hasn't been without trials, challenges, setbacks, and lots of internal struggle, *because it has been*—all of those and more, time after time. When I left the security of a steady paycheck and benefits, I faced all of the usual challenges most entrepreneurs encounter—the tremendous stress of a completely uncertain future, a complete overhaul of me and my family's lifestyle, and loads of pressure on my marriage and other vital relationships. In the early days, my mind was always in overdrive, always trying to close the next 'big deal,' and always striving to handle everything myself to save costs. The first year was intense and exhausting, and I was more energized than I'd ever been. It wasn't easy, but I kept at it—pitching a new model to manufacturers—one where I worked to find out how I could better serve them than their current distribution company. I asked lots of questions in the early days. I still do. Questions like:

What needs were not being met?

What services were missing that could enhance their processes?

What would help them better achieve their endgame for their products?

It took a lot of time upfront—more than I had ever previously been allowed to devote to a single potential client—

but I always knew there was a better way. My industry was overdue for some fresh thought, and I could provide that. But it was also met with some serious skepticism. In fact, one of the biggest obstacles I faced was trying to convince potential clients that my interest in a true partnership with them was genuine and not some gimmick. More than a few companies were suspicious of my inclusive model.

"Seriously? You know you're going to upset a whole lot of old school folks if you deliver everything you're telling me you're going to," one of my former employer's clients told me. And that was the beginning of what led me to become known as "the guy who turned the distribution business upside down."

My company primarily services a highly specialized niche, the luxury leather goods market, but the practices and service models we have become known for are universal. Just because we represent some of the most prestigious leather goods brands in the world—revered, highly-sought after names—our charge, at the end of the day, is still to help our clients achieve *their* goals and realize *their* vision for the products they produce. And something I learned from my earliest days in the industry that has stuck with me for almost three decades now, is that my clients are just like customers across all industries, at all levels—they simply want to be heard and respected for their input.

Beyond my first client, which I'll tell you about later on, I was able to convince a few companies to take a chance and see if I didn't live up to my promises. Before I knew it, word got out that my clients were doing better than they had ever done, moving merchandise quickly and efficiently and enjoying great success. It was a season of exciting new growth.

And then…then we landed *the big one*—one of the crown jewels in the luxury leather goods world. It was actually our *first* client, but because we had proved ourselves with small, initial orders, they rewarded us with the type of ongoing business that has driven us to amazing success. It was a tipping point for our company and confirmed to everyone involved in the distribution process that genuine partnerships—truly mutually beneficial collaborations, if you will—coupled with personalized programs, closely watched analytics, and a responsive sales rep were the missing links in a long-outdated business model.

After being awarded such a prestigious account, clients started *coming to us.* It was a complete game-changer for Jericho Enterprises. *And* it brought us to this defining moment in my life—the moment when my former boss, Barry Nettles, was front and center in *my* company's conference room, presenting to *my* brain trust—a cross-section of men and women from all levels within the company, and making his case for why our team should add his products to our respected client list.

shift

To each, there comes in their lifetime a special moment when they are figuratively tapped on the shoulder and offered the chance to do a very special thing, unique to them and fitted to their talents. What a tragedy if that moment finds them unprepared or unqualified for that which could have been their finest hour.

- Winston Churchill

chapter two

"Good morning, Jackie. Is the team ready to go?" I asked my first lieutenant Jackie Dixon. Jackie was the first hire I made when I started the company and has been invaluable on this journey. She has kept every*thing* and every*one* running around here since Day One.

"Everyone is on their way in right now; they're just refilling their coffee. Here—I grabbed one for you, too," she said as she took her regular seat to my right. "Boy, it's been a week. There were a few moments I thought Friday would never get here!"

"Well, this will be an interesting one…Barry is pitching next." "Good old Barry," she said with a smile. She knew the full backstory of Barry's role in my previous life. Barry had been my boss at my most recent former employer, Bowman + Leonard, where I languished for ten years under his autocratic leadership style in what I used to refer to as 'middle management hell.'

shift

Unfortunately for Barry, and the rest of our office back then, we had all been a victim of a hostile takeover six years earlier. Even being the brother-in-law of B + L's CEO wasn't enough to spare Barry his job at the time. Still, to his credit, he had landed one more position before closing out his career and had since switched sides in the retail industry. Now, instead of representing various product lines to retailers, he was representing one manufacturer *to distributors*. And that is how our paths came to cross today.

A moment later, the rest of the team arrived and took their seats. Even though none of us have ever had an official place to sit, we have always laughed that our conference is kind of like a church, as we usually sit in the same seats every time we get together. Jerry always sits next to John, who always sits across from Kevin and Beth, and so on.

I had gathered my personal 'Brain Trust' to kick off what we call 'Pitch Week' at Jericho Enterprises. For us, it was the one week of the year that demanded all hands on deck, and it was also a call to up our usual casual wear to sports coats or pantsuits out of respect for our visitors. I had learned years ago that having people from every aspect of the business involved in these crucial decisions made us a better business. Everyone—from order takers, buyers, managers, folks from the shipping department, and executives—all of them bring their job's perspective to the table. It just makes sense to get input from the people who are most impacted by the critical buying and selling decisions we make as a company. Hearing the way they view our potential products is one of my favorite aspects of the business.

The week also meant gearing up for 12-hour days of back-to-back appointments, one prospective vendor after another, as each tried to convince our team their products were a good fit for our current lines. Our track record for taking designers and innovators from obscurity to sought-after many times over in our brief six years had become well-known throughout the industry. It was also one of the most fulfilling aspects of what I now happily referred to as 'my job.'

The week was grueling and mind-numbing at times, but in the end, our team had unanimously decided it was considerably more efficient than the constant requests for appointments throughout the year by persistent sales reps. 'One and done' was how our Jericho crew referred to it—one week of intense and limited presentations, and we were done until next year.

From the beginning, I had made it a priority to end the week with generous gift cards for everyone involved—the executive team, admin assistants, and support staff—to some of Dallas' nicest restaurants for dinner Friday evening, in hopes that a nice dinner with a spouse or significant other might begin to compensate for the demanding week. Several mentors of mine showed me how far small acts could go towards reinforcing the value I placed on my team members. Even something as simple as a gift card reminded them their efforts were appreciated and not taken for granted.

The postmortem from pitch week was always held on the following Monday morning after having had the weekend to consider our options. Everyone came prepared with their individual recommendations, and we worked quickly through the selection process. Some options were obviously a good fit for us; others were apparently not up to standards; it was the ones somewhere in-between that usually brought the most discussion.

We quickly realized that, just because something was unique, didn't automatically mean it was acceptable. By the time we all left the conference room on Monday afternoon, our crew was a united team, usually having championed a few personal favorites and compromised on a few others. It made me immensely proud to see our company culture of such collaborative teamwork come through during these sessions. No doubt, it had taken a while to fully integrate in the beginning, but now it was apparent at every level within the organization. We welcomed new ways of looking at things, even outright disagreements that presented completely alternative perspectives, but once a decision was made, we unanimously rallied for it.

Now, here's where the movie moment comes in...

On the final day of Pitch Week, my now infamous former boss, Barry Nettles, was presenting. During his tenure at B + L, he came to be known as 'Barry-there-is-no-team-in-I.' Sure, it was immature, but it was also appropriate. He was 10 minutes into his team's presentation, and I had hardly heard a word. Their visuals were slick and impressive, their six-member team seemed suitably prepared, though not particularly engaging as the only one to speak was Barry, and their samples were nice, though nothing truly unique.

But there was a bigger disconnection between what Barry was pitching and what we were looking to buy. It wasn't just that his products were lacking innovative design so much as it was his approach to the whole manufacturer/distributor/retailer relationship. We saw it as a collaborative effort; he had always seen it as a fragmented, by-the-book, model. And for us, that was a deal-breaker.

Barry's was the type of pitch that elicited yawns from us all and was frequently forgotten before the reps caught the next elevator down. Still, we all worked to be respectful and receptive to everyone who had made an effort to prepare a presentation on our behalf. It was just good business to respect their efforts, and besides, our appointments had a 30-minute time limit. 'We can listen to anybody for 30 minutes,' was the motto we reminded each other as the days wore on.

Since the turnabout in our respective roles, Barry was fond of bragging about having trained me in the early years. "I taught him everything he knows!" Barry would frequently tell anyone who would listen at industry conferences and trade shows. He obviously felt responsible for my success.

I never corrected him—it wasn't worth the effort it would require to set him straight. But, every time I heard Barry's reference to our time spent together, I couldn't help but think, "Yeah, you taught me all right. Taught me to run from innovation and exploring new options, and taught me to keep my nose down, go by the book, and stick to the way things had always been done." If you really boiled it down, it was 'my way or the highway' as Barry used to say it.

shift

I will concede in Barry's defense; it was all Barry knew to do and therefore, all he knew to preach. He would always point out that it was his method that had landed the biggest account in the company's history, never mind that it was some 15 years ago. This moment of temporary and long-ago success had since led Barry to hang his hat upon the old adage, 'why change what works?' What he always failed to add was that, since his epic win, 'his way' hadn't brought in any other clients even half that size even in an expanding market.

As a result, at the time, it was all I knew, too, though I couldn't help but think there had to be a better way after decades of following the same practices and procedures, regardless of the client. If ever there was a poster boy for unimaginative, by-the-book presentations, Barry Nettles was it. He was a one-trick pony on autopilot, now more than ever, coasting until retirement.

As Barry begin to wrap up his presentation, I couldn't help but watch his junior exec take it all in. I usually am really good at remembering names, but when I realized it was Barry's company presenting, I knew I didn't have to remember the others as it would be *all Barry*. Still, one young man captured my interest. He was a young guy, maybe early 30s, and had yet to earn a speaking role under Barry's tutelage. I had spent too many years in this guy's position to not recognize his indifference and lack of follow-through on his assigned role. As a junior exec, he didn't have too many responsibilities during the pitch. Mostly, he was charged with nodding at the appropriate times, feigning a bit of enthusiastic interest at his boss' babble, and most importantly, read the room and assess how well his boss' message was being received. One glance at this fellow and it was clear—he wasn't buying what Barry was selling.

I leaned in to make out his name from his temporary badge. His name was Tom, and his body language was telegraphing far more than it should have been revealing. I'd been in Tom's position more times than I wanted to count and had to laugh at my amateur diagnosis: Either Tom strongly disagrees with what Barry is pitching, or his appendix is about to burst. I had a sense there was more to his story.

"And that, ladies and gentlemen, is why the exceptional purses and wallets from Schultzman & Company would be a tremendous asset to your company's fall/winter line…" Barry trailed off to the polite but subdued by the applause of our crew as I went to shake his hand and personally thank him.

"Barry, thank you for coming today. It's good to hear how your kids are doing, and now even grandkids! You must have done something right!" I offered. As our team was shaking hands and collecting samples, I noticed Tom was still at the conference table making some notes and shaking his head as if Barry had left something out, and he wished he could have done something about it.

That's what triggered me to do something pretty unusual for me and outside our usual protocol—I asked Barry if one of his team members could stay behind.

"I'd like to hold your guy, Tom, back for a bit? I've got a few questions I'd like to run past him. Don't feel like you need to wait on him; I'll arrange for a driver to get him back to the office as soon as we're done."

"Tom? But he's just a junior rep. I'd be happy to stay and answer anything you've got questions about. I oversaw the design and mock-ups of everything we presented today and can answer anything you…"

"I know, I know," I countered. "I think that's what interests me—his youth and relatively fresh perspective." I was working hard to choose my words carefully so as not to discredit Barry's seniority or create trouble for Tom later on, but it was too late. I could sense Barry's insecurities rising to the top as he called Tom forward for introductions. It was clear Barry felt slighted at the preference shown to Tom but didn't want to harm his company's chances for consideration in our distribution line.

"Tom, David's been at this for going on 30 years now and has become a trusted friend of mine and Schultzman. We go back quite a few years together, don't we, David?"

Barry couldn't help himself. The resentment was palpable in his voice. He was an old-school sales rep, came up through the ranks, had paid his dues, survived some lean times, and was now just biding his time. The last thing he wanted was for some young upstart to interfere with his final few years at the company, and yet, it was happening right before his eyes: I was choosing the kid over the veteran, and there was nothing he could do about it.

"Why yes, Barry, yes, we do. Tom, I was just telling Barry I'd like for you to hang back a bit and visit with me for a while. I promised Barry we'd take good care of you and get you back to the office before too long. Is that okay with you?"

"Well, s-s-sure," Tom answered, "as long as it's good with *the boss.*"

"Oh shoot, sure it is," Barry lied. "If it's good for our business with Jericho Enterprises, it's always good with me. Take your time, answer the man's questions, and we'll see you at the office later this afternoon. Sound good?"

"Thanks, Mr. Nettles," Tom replied.

I wanted to bring this awkward exchange to an end as soon as possible and began leading Barry towards the conference room door. He took the hint, pausing only briefly to give Tom a parting scowl on his way out.

———————————

I closed the door to the conference room to ensure our complete privacy and motioned for Tom to have a seat as I took mine. "First off, thank you for your willingness to stay after and visit with me personally. Your team's new designs are nice enough and come in at our most popular price points. However, it's not that your company's products don't meet our criteria, it's just that your company's approach to developing substantial relationships with our clients is what seems to be lacking.

"I took the liberty to make a few observations during Barry's presentation and wondered if I might run them past you and ask a few questions along the way, too."

"Certainly, but Barry is really the one to…"

"I know, I know. I apologize if I put you in an uncomfortable position just now, but I didn't want to go behind Barry's back in making contact with you, and I just didn't see any other way around it. Barry's heart is generally in the right place, but I know he's prone to discount new ideas. I'm sure he's good with you having a little extra time to visit with me." I was trying to sell my last comment with a smile but didn't believe it myself. Tom didn't either, but I pressed on.

"So, I couldn't help but notice during Barry's presentation; you seemed less than enthusiastic. In fact, I could swear I saw you almost grimace when he started sharing the proposed new line. Am I too far off base? Are you hesitant about what was presented today?"

The silence in the room was stark. Tom was processing the ask as fast as he could and quickly realized there was a lot on the line depending upon his response. I had nothing to lose over this line of questions, and he had *everything* to lose. I could tell he was weighing his options—loyalty to Barry or potentially seizing a new opportunity? Either way, he knew he was going to need to have his story straight by the time he returned to the office.

"Listen, Barry knows this line, this company, this industry, like few others. He oversaw this new line from concept to sample stage. I-I-I mean it's not particularly groundbreaking style, but it has the makings of a good, solid product line with a substantial range of price points. We worked long and hard to meet the criteria your team asked for and bring our best product forward. This is Barry's baby, and he let us know early on he was the one with the history with your company."

"That's my point exactly, Tom! Almost all of what we consider to be the world's most outstanding products are the result of a collaborative effort. No one person can understand all the nuances of tailoring a product to best meet the needs of their intended target market. That's true for everything from cell phones to running shoes to finely crafted leather goods.

"All of us bring our experiences and perceptions to the table in a new product's infancy. You might see a purse intended for this type of woman with this set of needs; I could see it targeted for another type, with a whole different set of likes and dislikes. When we talk it through and hear each other's arguments, our perspectives are broadened and clarified. When we consider the opinions of others at this stage, we either become convinced of our ideas, or we come to see and appreciate that there are other, valid options. Working in a vacuum, or at least to the exclusion of others' honest input, doesn't serve anyone any good. Wouldn't you agree?"

"Well, sure. That's just common sense, but Barry has a handle on the market and…"

"Tom—you're not hearing what I'm saying and asking of you. Look, I get the whole loyalty to your company, not wanting to undermine your boss and I respect that wholeheartedly. Loyalty is one of our core values at Jericho Enterprises, so you've got to know I can appreciate the situation I've put you in. I've been in your shoes many times over. You find yourself being the 'yes' man to your boss' ideas. And if I'm guessing correctly, you've probably voiced your differing opinion several times in the past but were shut down even before you explained yourself. Am I right?"

shift

Tom couldn't help but chuckle and nod.

"And if you haven't already, you're probably looking to start a family, you're juggling a mortgage, car payments, and all types of other expenses that are keeping you right where you are. It's been more than a few years, buddy, but I have been where you are living *right now*. I've been the one playing the second chair to my boss' ideas. I've been the one getting a read on how good the pitch is going. I've been the one whose job it was during these types of presentations to pile on to whatever was being offered, ad-libbing on cue, working every trick up my sleeve to keep the mood upbeat even in a room full of blank stares. You have got to know…I have been in your shoes and stayed there waaaaaaaay too long. But there is a better way. A much better way."

I could tell Tom was at a crucial crossroads, wanting to answer me honestly but understandably hesitant to betray his boss. I knew I needed to respect his position and asked permission before going on. When he agreed, I continued.

"Even above loyalty here, we value trust. And that's because, without it, we're no better off collectively than individually. If we can't trust one another to show them our authentic selves—all of our offbeat ideas, different insights, contrary opinions, without fear of rubber stamped denial, we might as well close up shop and let everyone operate their own company of one."

I could sense he was beginning to feel more comfortable with me and that my interest was genuine and well-intended for his sake. "I am giving you my word, Tom, not a word of this will leave this room. This a completely off-the-record conversation."

He nodded slowly.

"Good. Now, I want to know *your* opinion of the samples presented today. Would you feel proud to say you worked on these? Is this the best effort of your company? If you were in charge, how would this presentation have played out and these samples differed? I know this is off-the-cuff, and you're not fully prepared, but surely you had an opinion on some of these samples."

"Well, actually," Tom began, "I did have a few sketches of my own. They're on my phone."

I couldn't help but smile at the familiarity of Tom's situation—he was living my life 20 years prior. I had to share my story and give him the opportunity to save him from spending the next 20 years waiting for something to change like I did.

"Tom, see that poster on the wall?" I pointed to a large framed print that featured artistically arranged words and phrases. "The words on that poster have guided me and everyone here who has chosen to leverage these principles against the challenges we all face. Those principles have formed the foundation of my life for the past five years and the life of my company. They represent how I came to learn the power of making successful transitions that can change the trajectory of your life for the better." I knew I was making a grand promise, but I also knew I had the goods to back it up. "Would you like to hear that story?

"I would be honored to hear it." Tom had made a decision; he was all in.

"Great. Now we're getting somewhere…" I thought to myself as I pulled my chair closer.

shift

Guilt, regret, resentment,
grievances, sadness, bitterness,
and all forms of non-forgiveness
are caused by too much past,
and not enough presence.

— Eckhart Tolle

chapter three

My career started as an intern at a Dallas company, The Huntington Group, the summer before I graduated college with a degree in management. At the time, I was grateful for the experience and to have a worthy addition to my resume. When all of my grandiose plans for joining a consulting firm in New York straight out-of-school fell through, I felt like my only option was to accept the ongoing offer few Huntington Group interns were extended. It was a good offer, but in many ways, it felt like I was giving up on my dreams. Jenny and I were heading towards marriage by then, and I knew her parents would appreciate and expect gainful employment from their future son-in-law. It was a job, a placeholder, something to hold me over in the short run, I told myself.

"I'll get some experience, maybe a promotion or two, sock away some money, and be golden in a couple of years," I said to

shift

myself in the beginning. After all, the gig came with a company car, benefits, a 401k, and a path to the coveted stock options— all the trappings of adulthood I was most definitely not ready to embrace just three weeks past graduation.

Wasn't it just last month I had won the dart tournament at O'Malley's?

And was enjoying free beer for a week?

And waking up 10 minutes before psych class *at noon*?

The changes those first few weeks of out-of-school rocked my world. But after seeing too many friends struggling to land a job, I decided maybe I was ahead of the curve after all. So, I managed to rally, bought a few professional clothes, and gave it all I had. The plan was to leave this first job in my rearview mirror in one year, maybe two. Maximum.

Before I knew it, two years had turned into six, and by then, Jenny and I were fully entrenched in all the trappings of suburban life—the very thing I had so desperately wanted to avoid as a younger man. As a husband, and then a father to a two-year-old with another on the way, the reality of my growing responsibilities was hard to ignore. By the time I factored in a mortgage, a car payment, and Jenny's nearby parents in failing health, I knew the whole New York City dream would remain just that—a dream.

I discovered pretty quickly that the politics at Huntington were going to be a challenge and if I had any hope of advancement, I needed to get on board with 'the company way.' I quickly fell in line, started accepting the status quo, and eventually shelved my entrepreneurial dreams. 'Someday' was beginning to seem more and more unattainable with each passing year that I was working for someone else.

Eventually, I did mix it up a bit on the career front, though nothing substantial. I stayed in the same industry and just switched companies. I was looking for hope on all fronts. I wanted, and desperately needed, an increase in salary. I had given a lot of thought about my career path and wanted a company I could work my way up through. And just as important as the financial and career progression were to me, I was also in pressing need of finding a more collaborative work environment—one where my opinion carried some weight, and upper management was open to trying new concepts.

I broadened my search beyond the Dallas/Ft. Worth area to include the entire state. As long as Jenny could hop a plane back to Dallas on a moment's notice from another metropolitan area in the state, she was open to moving. I shopped my resume to companies in Houston, Austin, and San Antonio, and I had a few discreet meetings with a several of our competitors at out-of-the-way Starbucks to test the waters.

In the end, a move wasn't necessary. We remained exactly where we had been the last six years.

Same house.

Same street.

Same neighborhood.

Same *everything*.

shift

From the outside, the sameness of our lives at least *appeared* good. We managed to keep the girls in a good private school, were current on our bills, and weren't carrying any debt beyond our house and car. Admittedly, it was a better lifestyle than many enjoyed, but my inner turmoil behind the scenes didn't match up with the picture-perfect family. I wanted my next job to be the one to get me back on track to the lifestyle everyone thought I already had.

I settled on joining the team at our biggest competitor, Bowman + Leonard. No doubt, B + L was a step-up from The Huntington Group—larger, more prestigious, and with a higher grade of goods to represent, but ultimately, it was more of the same.

"Same song, different verse," my college buddies scolded me when I first shared the news. I took it good-naturedly, but I was thinking the same thing too.

B + L said all the right things in the beginning. The promise of a reasonably quick career progression and a fair increase in base pay and commission percentages was enough to justify pulling the trigger on a career jump. And honestly, my first few years there actually seemed promising to some degree. I had negotiated a respectable compensation arrangement from the start. Personally, though, I was working mostly on uninspired projects and courting small-time businesses. Still, my numbers were sufficient enough to earn a few promotions, some additional responsibilities, and a small team of junior execs to manage. The relationships with my team came to be the best part of my job.

Upper management took notice of my team's work ethic and willingness to help one another, even when they had nothing to gain from it. It was almost a foreign concept to some of the more territorial supervisors, but it was intriguing enough to be named the head of the Midwest sales division.

For a time, I felt my entrepreneurial spirit had come alive again. I was re-energized at the thought of actually moving the needle in what was frequently referred to as 'the flat, uneventful, and weakest link in the ranks of the B + L regions.' I saw the promotion as a chance to implement change, at least within my region. I read up on every leadership and management book I could get my hands on. I drafted a set of guidelines to encourage and inspire and empower my increased sales territory and the team that went with it. I even foolishly thought I might change the model for how we serviced our clients, pitched new business, and even grew and developed our team members.

And then, eight years into my time at B + L, *everything changed,* and my career progression came to a screeching halt.

No sooner had I called together my team to share my new vision and plans for our region, then it was announced that Barry Nettles, the brother-in-law of the B + L CEO, was being brought in by company leadership to light a fire under what he called "a pathetic and lackluster" team of sales representatives. Barry was charged with overseeing the North American distribution group which meant all of the regional heads, myself included, would all be reporting to him until "somebody brought in some decent sales figures" as Barry put it.

shift

Barry's position would require a good bit of travel between the regions, but unfortunately for our team, he had chosen to make Dallas his home base because of his affinity for "those damn Dallas Cowboys" as he called them. It wasn't long into Barry's tenure before those of us in the Dallas office quickly learned to predict the tenor of Mondays based upon the showing by 'America's Team' on Sunday afternoon.

Barry came at his new position as he said, "With guns blazing," never hesitant to remind everyone he was in charge. He was a barrel-chested, weather-worn 50-something man known as much for his girth as his thundering persona. He often used his convenient marriage to the CEO's sister as leverage whenever he wanted to assert his authority. His management style could be summed up in one word: intimidation. He was quick to call my ideas about customer service "all that feel good relationship crap" as he referred to it, a waste of time and pointed to his decades of sales experience whenever his methods were questioned.

In all his years in the field, he boasted there weren't too many accounts he hadn't been able to land after a few rounds of scotch or whiskey with the right people. "Nobody says 'no' to a single malt," he preached. "And nobody says 'no' to Barry Nettles after a few rounds of stout whiskey."

Sales had always increased whenever Barry was brought in to a company. There was no denying he got results, at least in the short run. He would usually get some big order on the books and leverage that to get other new clients, but retention usually plummeted dramatically within a year of his arrival—a fact that was somehow glossed over by bravado whenever he joined a new firm.

To say that he was intolerant of new methods, procedures, and sales approaches were the understatement of the century. His unofficial slogan was "profits first, people second," and he lived it out in everything he did. It was 'his way or the highway,' and everyone who crossed him learned this the hard way. The crew at B + L was no exception as each of us had, in turn, tried different approaches to win him over in his early days at the company. We all fared pretty much the same—we each failed miserably.

Unfortunately, I was the first regional manager to get into a tangle with him soon after he came on board. I knew Barry was a veteran in the industry but knew little else besides that. I had asked around before he started with B + L, but few of his contacts were willing to share their honest opinion of him. Instead, they used words like 'intense' and 'focused' and 'numbers-focused,'— all terms that could be a great asset.

Or a stifling character flaw.

At first, I took these descriptions to be positive indications for potential improvements to B + L's long outdated way of doing business. I even had visions of learning how to best manage my team, how to better serve our clients, and possible introductions to new clients he could provide.

I couldn't have been more wrong.

What I had first thought to be a new opportunity and a chance to update our old sales model ultimately turned out to be the death knell for my advancement as long as Barry Nettles was in charge. I had made an impression all right; just not the one I intended to.

Barry's first week on the job, I scheduled a face-to-face with him. "Get in there early, show him what I've got, and make a good impression from the start," I told myself. In the days before my appointment with him, I worked night and day on the best way to present my new ideas. By the time of the appointment, I was comfortable and confident when I walked into his office.

My enthusiasm was short-lived as soon as I realized my proposal went against everything Barry knew and practiced. "Let me get this straight, Jericho," I can still remember him saying, "you want to offer more...*more*...MORE customer service to these skinflints haggling over a percentage or two? And oh, by the way, you want to stagger your commission in hopes of 'landing the big one' somewhere down the road with these people?

"Are you trying to give away the whole company? I don't know about you, but I'm kind of used to receiving a regular paycheck...*not a deferred one*. Operate like that too long, and there won't be any commission to negotiate."

When he paused to catch his breath, I wanted to make a break for it but knew there was no escaping this verbal beat down.

"I tell you what, float that past your people in the field—getting a paycheck sometime in the future in lieu of *now*. See how well that goes over. In the meantime, your Midwest people had best make their numbers, or it falls on you." I wanted to correct him and clarify his misunderstanding of my ideas, but something told me not to rock the boat any further than I already had. It was a lost cause, and I was a beaten man at that point.

After that, I was never considered an all-out company man. My ill-received 'give-more-to-get-more' pitch had branded me more client-focused than company-focused—a cardinal sin at B + L. Barry could never get past the short-sightedness of my plan even after all these years. He repeatedly made excuses about me not being a strong enough leader or hard-hitting enough to snag one of the coveted east or west coast regions. As a result, I began defaulting into the habit of keeping my ideas to myself and towing the proverbial company line.

Occasionally, I would indulge my inner entrepreneur and imagine things in a "Jericho" world setting—the one where I could make the calls about business practices and team engagement. I kept an ongoing file of my ideas; ironically named 'Someday.'

In my diminishing moments of inspiration, I would still occasionally pull together a hypothetical pitch and envision how things would play out if I were ever to assume Barry's role. "Oh, the changes I would make," I used to imagine. Most days, however, the tyranny of the urgent kept me addressing my team and my clients and left me with little mental bandwidth to consider such possibilities.

It was in the quieter moments of my life, usually on the drive home, that the 'what if' demons crept into my consciousness. I'd do battle with them, tell myself I had responsibilities that didn't allow for such an indulgence, and file them away 'til the next time they appeared. Lately, however, I couldn't help but notice

shift

the one word that kept surfacing whenever I gave into the 'what if' thoughts: settled.

Several years back, in a moment of brutally honest self-reflection, I had come to terms with my life *as it was*, not as I had envisioned it playing out. The revelation was startling and sobering; the reality undeniable. I had held such hope, such promise for my life. Instead, I admitted, I had *settled*.

I had taken the first job I could get right out of school *and settled*.

I had considered career leaps, cross-country relocations, but in the end, family pressures and obligations had prevailed, and *I had settled*.

I had quit engaging in social media exchanges with most of my friends and didn't even know why. And then I realized it was because I was ashamed because *I had settled*.

"It's just like how all those people referred to Barry when I asked about him," I thought to myself. "All those descriptors were accurate. I just stupidly accepted them to mean something positive, something hopeful, something promising and they were anything but that. It's the same for me—I used to think *settled* meant comfortable, stable, secure. Now, all it means is that I was a sucker for staying put for so long—too long—and not taking any chances."

As the years wore on, my submissions to the 'Someday' file became less and less frequent. I eventually resigned myself to accepting the culture of B + L as it was, with little hope for significant change until Barry retired. My dreams of affecting company culture had all but disappeared as I ultimately began to realize the situation I had gotten myself into and the circumstances I was facing.

My once hopeful outlook had all but evaporated. The absence of any indication of significant change on the horizon felt defeating. My association with B + L had become a job, not the promising career path I had first hoped it to be. It paid the bills, the taxes, and a few luxuries, but ultimately, it was little more than a means to an end.

Year by year, Barry's influence was more and more evident as fewer and fewer of the employees remained from his first days with the company. For whatever reason—one I can't even answer fully myself, I chose to stay, hoping against hope to ride out the storm that was known as Barry Nettles.

shift

Sometimes, our lives have to be completely shaken up, changed, and rearranged to relocate us to the place we need to be.

-Unknown

chapter four

I was 18 years in at B + L by now and standing in front of a packed ballroom, accepting a pathetic award for length of service. It was my third of such honor based solely on tenure, not merit. In recent years, company leadership had consistently opted not to single any one employee out for outstanding service, choosing instead to have all employees completing 15-20 years of service stand for a collective round of applause. It was safest that way, HR had recommended. No possible discrimination issues, no accusations of favoritism, no ill feelings from those overlooked. Factual and verifiable years of service had become the default for recognition.

"Eighteen years at one company and I'm sharing the moment with Ned in Receiving and Margaret from Accounting," I thought while forcing a grin when they called my name. I made

shift

it up to the front to claim my faux wood plaque with a polished brass plastic plate bearing my name and years of service. I truly felt like Dwight Schrute, from *The Office*, winning the Best Assistant Manager "Dundie" and dedicating it to the trash can.

"C'mon, Jericho. You can do better than that," the presenting EVP chided me as we shook hands and posed for the photograph. And that was the extent of my company's landmark recognition for the last 18 years of my life.

By the next Friday, I had moved past what I thought to be a pathetic show of appreciation for my years of service. It was Friday, after all, and I had a reunion with my closest college buddies this weekend to look forward to. The plan was to get through the day, maybe even leave a bit early, and surprise Jenny with a dinner out. Eight hours until two days of freedom.

I pulled into my usual parking spot, flashed my badge at the security guard, and headed towards the elevators. On the way in, I passed one of our newest junior sales reps on his way out of the building.

"Sorry, man," the young guy said as he brushed past me in a hurry. And then as if to explain his urgency, he turned halfway around and continued to walk partially backward. "You know how once in a while somebody starts talking about buying us out? This time, it's for real. The guys at Southwest Capital have found some serious money—some Chinese company is backing them, and word is on the street is that the deal is going through… before the end of the quarter."

I didn't even have time to react before he was out the revolving glass doors. "He's new," I thought to myself. "This happens every few years, and nothing ever comes of it. We get all worked up, the bankers come to look at the books, and the deal always falls apart. Poor guy—getting all worked up over nothing."

But by the time I reached my floor and swung open the double glass doors leading into Bowman + Leonard, *I knew*. This time, it was different. *Really* different. It felt like a gigantic vacuum had sucked the energy out of the sea of cubicles. There was no morning chatter between the sales reps, no sports talk, no trading weekend plans between the young singles. The Friday feel-good vibes had apparently called in sick for the day.

As head of a region, I had eventually earned my own office, and *I loved it*. Gone were the days of overhearing guys trying to make up with their girlfriends or stressed-out parents frantically lining up carpool when babysitters called in sick. It had been a long time in coming, but I relished the escape of an actual office with a door. It was a retreat when some of the office politics and pettiness became an issue…which was *always*. Our culture of 'survival of the fittest' created tension and lack of trustworthiness among most coworkers. I did my best to counter this atmosphere within my group, but these distractions still surfaced now and then.

As I walked towards my office, my whole team seemed to avoid eye contact with me. "Hey guys, what's up? Why so tense this early? It's Friday!" I asked the group at large.

shift

"Ummm David, I think you need to talk to Barry," said one of my reps who was brave enough to speak up. "Or check your email."

No sooner had I set my briefcase down than I heard Barry ranting and pounding his desk. Two offices over. With my door closed.

I opened my email and got the first indication this potential buyout had some legs. The first thing I saw was a red-flagged email marked 'URGENT—IMPORTANT AND CONFIDENTIAL.'

Dear Staff –

Due to SEC regulations, we are informing you that a hostile offer has been made by Xi Chang LTD through their proxy, Southwest Capital. They have indicated their intent to secure 51% of Bowman + Leonard stock. While this move is not totally unexpected, the Board of Directors, working in close alignment with the senior management team, is working diligently to head off this effort.

I am restricted in what I can offer you by way of written communications, but will be holding meetings with senior executives who will then disseminate the appropriate information for your department and area of work as it relates to this matter. There will be an emergency meeting of all employees, regional directors and above, at 2:00 p.m. CST, with your appropriate EVP in your office's conference room.

Our desire and first priority is to remain independent and we will fight this effort with all of the resources we have, including our greatest resource, you—our employees.

I know that together we will prevail.

Onward together,
Edwin Younger
CEO, Bowman + Leonard

I scanned the email as quickly as possible as words like 'hostile' and 'fight' jumped off the screen. We had been warned of potential takeovers throughout the years, but we had never been in such a weak position to make the threat real. No one had gotten this far before or seemed like such a viable threat. I raced through the bullet points and landed on the details of what I interpreted to be a 'last-ditch emergency sales meeting' later in the day. As I reread the email, I sank into my chair, stunned by the news.

Unfortunately for the rest of us, Barry was as surprised as the rest of us. This was the first incident since his arrival at the company where his connection to the CEO was irrelevant, and he knew it. This time, it was as real for him as it was for all of us, and the tension in the office reflected it.

"This is unbelievable. I go from regretting spending my entire career here to all of a sudden hoping I can hang on for dear life just to keep my benefits and paycheck coming in," I thought. It was bizarre and surreal and overwhelming—all at the same time.

For better for worse, at the moment, I didn't have much time to process what the potential personal implications this might mean for my family and me because my staff had already done so for themselves. Within minutes, several of my sales reps were crowded into my office, firing one question after another, each understandably concerned about what this possibility meant for them.

"I just bought a new car *last month*! I can't make the payments without a job!"

"My kid's getting his tonsils out next week—I can't go without insurance."

"Do you know what the job market is like out there *now*? We'll never all find a job at the same time!"

I had to pull it together quickly for the sake of my team. I knew keeping them busy was important at this point because it would help to temper the anxiety in all of us and give us a sense of doing something proactive. "Get me your individual projections for this quarter…no, no…through the end of the fiscal year," I told them. "If you have so much as sent an email or talked to a prospective customer, include them on your forecast sheets. Don't lie, but don't leave anybody off, either. And expenses… nobody spends anything without prior approval from this point on. Don't even consider turning in expense reports till this thing blows over and then…then we'll take care of you."

"We've been here before," I lied to them. We'd never actually been this close before, but I didn't see any good in sharing that tidbit of historical data. "There have been rumors in the past, but we've always been able to fight them off. This time is no exception. We can do this. Let's make the Midwest region the linchpin in the survival of Bowman + Leonard."

They all seemed satisfied for the moment. They may not have believed me any more than I believed myself, but the assignment would keep their hands and heads busy for a couple of hours, and we all needed that. I took my own advice and got to work, gathering my numbers too—both the actual ones and a few possibly overly optimistic ones as well. I told myself I'd follow through and make these accounts happen after this blew over.

By early afternoon, I had reports from all my team. They were adequate, but not especially outstanding. Still, it was something to present and stand behind for the 2:00 meeting with Stan Levinger, our division's EVP. I had worked through lunch, too nauseous to eat, pulling together any and everything I thought would offer hope.

At 1:55, I had what I hoped to be an admirable forecast for the Midwest region. I gathered my reports and suit coat and headed for the conference room where I was expecting to hear the actual outlook concerning the long-term viability of the company I'd sunk almost two decades of my life into. I was also expecting a game plan from company leadership about how they intended to keep us all employed and continue to operate as an independent business.

shift

I grossly overestimated the depth of their plans.

"I'll make this short and sweet," Levinger led with, "because our time is best spent acting, not discussing. Our only chance to avoid this takeover is to secure a major—MAJOR—new client. I'm talking stratosphere-level of a new client. The account needs to bring in half a million unit sales at the minimum. If there's any prospect you've ever considered approaching, now is the time. If somebody owes you a favor, call it in NOW. Anything less and everything and everyone are on the line. Now, get at it!"

And just like that, the meeting was over.

I could hardly grasp what had just happened. Had I misunderstood what Stan had just said?

Where is the strategy in this? The questions in my mind were coming me in rapid-fire succession.

What about brainstorming?

Isn't combining forces and openly discussing solutions one of the fundamental practices of effective teamwork?

I was caught up in the lunacy of this scatter-gun approach. Had Barry or Stan honestly never read *a single book* on effective leadership? Identifying a top-tier client and pitching their management team and winning their break-the-bank business was near impossible for a truly dynamic team. It was insane and utterly unacceptable for an individual to even consider. I knew it, and my team would recognize it immediately too.

I made my way back to my office and closed the door. I had to think this through before facing my team with this ridiculous charge. In my mind, all I could think was, "This is the end. This is truly the end." I ran through the litany who I was going to disappoint when the wheels fell off the B + L bus. "This is the end of my life as I know it. I'm 46 years old, I've got another half dozen years of college tuition for the girls, Jenny's dad to move into a nursing home within the year, and another ten years left on the house note. And this is how it ends. This is what it means to feel utterly and completely hopeless."

shift

The deepest fear we have, 'the
fear beneath all fears,' is the
fear of not measuring up,
the fear of judgment. It's this
fear that creates the stress
and depression of everyday life.

–Tullian Tchividjian

chapter five

"Don't forget your sweatshirt," Jenny yelled from the kitchen.

I knew the one she was referring to—it was one of the last remaining items from our days in college. It was the one my roommates and I had worn for our last picture together just before graduation. Across the front, it read: 'The Tenement Crew' in block university-style letters. One of the guy's moms had them printed for Christmas during our senior year as a reference to the dilapidated old home we had shared throughout our last three years in school. It hadn't been condemned when we lived there, but it was close enough and cheap.

Almost every memory from my college days could be traced to my time with The Tenement Crew. "Remember when Jack rode a horse through the downstairs and she started eating the couch?" The horse story was a perennial favorite, especially the part about how the old mare left a deposit on her way out the back door, and somebody's then-girlfriend stepped on it and ran out of the house crying. "She should have known better than to wear sandals in that house!"

"And how about the time Sam's girlfriend filled the upstairs bathtub with instant mashed potatoes, and it sat there the whole time we were gone for Spring Break! We thought somebody had died when we walked in. I bet they never got rid of that stench."

"Wonder if Old Man Jackson still lives across the street and calls the cops every time somebody parks in front of his house? I thought when we offered to mow his yard that time he might let up, but no such luck. I wonder if he ever realized the cookies Julie took over as a peace offering had Ex-Lax in them!"

The stories never got old. Every reunion, somebody would lead with one "remember when" story and we'd be off and running, laughing and embellishing till the early morning hours. It always did our group good to reminisce about our shared history and catch up with what was currently going on in each other's lives.

Since graduation, all six of us had a standing agreement to get together every other year on the first weekend in November for an informal reunion. We all went to great lengths not to miss the reunion—it was that important to us. Four out of six of us were still with our first wives; the other two were both in serious relationships but in no rush to make it official. Two of our wives had graduated with us, including Jenny, and the other two married into the group within a few years of graduation. All of our wives and girlfriends had become fast friends and kept up with one another through social media, Christmas cards, and the occasional group text.

Every time our group got together, we made it a point to bring our matching sweatshirts and snap a picture somewhere on campus before the weekend was over. Though everybody was still relatively fit and in good health, the years were becoming increasingly more evident whenever we compared the original picture with the newest one.

"I got it," I yelled back, and started mumbling to myself. "There's gotta be a flame-out in every group and guess who drew *that* short straw? That's right, friends, David Jericho, the one who was going to conquer the world; the one who seemed to have the world by the tail, the one who…"

"Were you talking to me?" Jenny was standing in the doorway.

"Uh, no. I was, uh, just thinking out loud," I started. "Listen, I know we talked about this last night, but I just don't know that I've got it in me to act like everything's all great in our world right now. I mean compared to the other guys, a bad day for them is when the price of fuel for their plane goes up or their personal concierge calls in sick."

I was referring to the recent buy-in by one of the guys who had purchased partial ownership in a Citation X because, as Pete said, "Those commercial planes are like cattle calls these days." Everyone in the group had also done exceptionally well financially—*everyone but me*. Pete was heading up a mid-size

shift

hedge fund; Don just celebrated making partner in his company with a trip to Barcelona; Sam had taken over his family's business and was thriving; Sid and Charlie had gone into business together, creating a chain of used car dealerships that financed loans to high-risk individuals at exorbitant rates. That way of making a living wasn't something I could get on board with ethically, but I had to admit the return on investment was tremendously lucrative and sometimes tempting.

It's not like I begrudged my friends for their successes; I truly didn't. They had each worked hard, taken significant chances in the last ten years, and now, they all appeared to be reaping tremendous rewards financially and otherwise. In fact, if I was honest with myself, it wasn't so much that they were doing so well that bothered me, it was that compared to them, I wasn't even in the same ballpark. I had become 'the company guy' who had spent too many years in middle management hell at B + L. It was what I knew, and up until today, where I assumed I would remain until retirement.

"Jenny, I don't know that you understand how devastating this potential buyout could be for us, and the pressure—oh my God—the pressure I feel to land the biggest account of my life and make sure my team keeps their jobs—*that* pressure is suffocating," I was trying unsuccessfully not to sound overly desperate.

"But David, I don't need all that stuff—the private plane, the European getaways, the..." Jenny started in before I interrupted her.

"Don't you get it? That stuff is the scorecard! It's the benchmark for what people consider success. These guys all have it, and I'm not even close."

"But you know as well as I do that it hasn't always been this way," Jenny's voice of reason was throwing a wrench in what I feared to be my new reality. "These guys just followed their passion early on, but it wasn't without lots of trials and setbacks. Heck, Charlie and Rebecca's marriage fell apart over his first start-up. And Sid filed for bankruptcy just five years ago. They're just now making big money.

"If some of those guys' starts and restarts don't prove that you can move forward from here, I don't know what will. If *they* can do it, there's no doubt you can too. And besides, the hotel is already paid for, and if things are as dire as you make them out to be, we may not be getting away from home for a very long time. It always does us good to spend the weekend with this crew. And maybe one of the guys might have some connection for that big account you're looking for—it could actually be good for your business."

Jenny was pressing hard, but for me, the reunion was indeed the last place on earth I wanted to be. But I also knew Jenny had a valid point—it could quite possibly be our last get-away for a very long time.

"I give," I conceded. "I'll be ready in 10 minutes."

The three-hour drive back to school was like hitting auto-play for us. Between the two of us, we had driven the roads back and forth so many times throughout the years, both as students

shift

and now as alumni, that we used to laugh we could make the drive with our eyes closed.

Jenny had downloaded a movie to her iPad and was well into it before we hit the interstate. I was grateful she had brought the earbuds and wasn't looking to rehash our discussion from the night before. I had laid out what the probable buyout would mean for us—best case, things would continue as they were, possibly for the short-term, though probably not forever; more likely though, I explained I was anticipating a full sweep of the management positions, mine included, with probably little more than a couple of month's severance.

I knew it wasn't that Jenny didn't grasp the magnitude of the repercussions; she did. It was just that she was actively choosing 'not to borrow trouble' as she put it. The crazy thing is, it was this overly optimistic outlook that had first attracted me to her almost 20 years ago. She always had faith in God and me—no matter what. This time was no exception; she had absolute faith we would be okay, no matter what. For once, I wanted her to lose the rose-colored glasses and face what I assumed to be our new, desperate reality.

My mind ran the gamut during the drive back to school as I was forced to accept every aspect of my life was up for grabs. I mulled over the past, the present, and certainly, the future. I thought of some of my past business start-up dreams and how I had never followed through on a single one of them. I ran through my client list, wondering who might hire me. I started a mental list of our biggest competitors that I could approach and then moved on to my network of connections that might open a few doors.

One of the biggest hurdles I knew we would face as a family would be the loss of benefits—not the least of which was a company car. Between the loss of health insurance for us all and giving up the company car and gas card, I knew I'd be facing a heavy hit for having to make an early withdrawal from my 401k. I even went so far as to consider the payout on my life insurance policy and calculated how far I thought it might carry Jenny and the girls.

Jenny interrupted my desperate thoughts, "Honey, don't you need to be in the right-hand lane to catch the next exit?"

"Oh yeah. Sorry, lost in thought for a sec. Thanks for catching that."

Within minutes, we were on campus after stopping at the College Inn to drop our bags off before meeting up with our crew for lunch at O'Malley's, the longstanding student pub known for the coldest beer in town and half-price burgers during finals week. More than just a few undergrads had drowned their sorrows after a particularly fierce round of finals, myself included.

"Get in here," Don yelled as we crossed the threshold of the door and allowed our eyes to adjust. "How the hell are ya'll? I was starting to wonder if you guys were going to make it." The other couples had all gotten there within the last hour and had already started catching up. We made our way through the hugs and kisses of everyone before taking the last two remaining chairs at the table.

shift

"So, we're way ahead of you with what's going on with us. What is happening at the Jericho household?" Sid asked. Sid was one half of the high-interest car dealership team and always the biggest risk taker of the group. Not only had he made a lot at the expense of the credit-poor, but he had also invested in a few biotech start-ups that had just gotten FDA approval on a signature product and was enjoying the meteoric rise in their stock price. "You holding everything together at B + L?"

"Well, funny you should bring that up," I said as I eased into my grim prospects. "Turns out the guys at Southwest Capital were able to arrange some serious financing from the Xi Chang group and are making a run at buying us out. We've had others come at us through the years, but this time, I think it may just go through."

"But you've got stock options by now, right?" asked Pete. "So, the buyout should set you up nicely."

I did everything I could to mask my disappointment at what Pete assumed to be fact. Knowing I was one management level short of receiving substantial stock options was another blow to my financial future. Another shortfall. I felt like I had to compensate for my missed-it-by-an-inch seniority level and the potential benefits one level higher could have provided.

"The stock's so low right now; it wouldn't be worth much anyway. But we're still in the middle of figuring out what that might mean for us. In fact, we just got the word yesterday that I, rather we—the whole B + L team—is in deep, deep need of landing a huge account—probably bigger than I've ever snagged—if any of us want to keep our jobs and possibly head off the takeover. And chances of that are…" I didn't need to finish my sentence; the crestfallen faces staring back at me were jolting enough. "Man, can I bring a party down like a rock star or what?"

A few of the guys managed an uneasy chuckle. "But seriously, guys, we're not going to let some no-name hedge fund ruin the weekend, are we? Besides, I'm starting to think Jenny's idea about not borrowing trouble might be the way to go."

"But David, Xi Chang is not some no-name group. They are known for being the most ruthless, take-no-prisoners, kind of team out there. Surely, you remember how they gutted Seros Technology. Or SoftBox Toys. Or…" Charlie stopped himself before going on.

"But, what's my choice, guys? Land the account of a lifetime and get to keep doing more of the same or lose my job entirely and the almost 20 years I've poured into it. It's not like I've got too many viable options right now." It took everything within me to keep my voice calm and steady.

"Yeah, but David, you are *the guy*. You were the one, out of all of us, who was set on conquering the business world. Remember how Professor Morgan used *your* management case study as 'the example' for what a project should look like? Remember how you were the one chosen to represent the business college by Dean Robertson whenever we were up for accreditation? You couldn't stop talking about the ideas and angles and all types of new concepts you had in mind for how you'd launch a company that would change the world, and use your success to impact some remote village in India or some other God forsaken place. When you signed on with The Huntington Group, you were the only guy they gave a signing bonus to. You were gonna get in there, show 'em what you were made of, pay your dues, and jump ship to a bigger and more innovative place after you had some experience under your belt. You even talked about going out on your own before you turned 30 and made a name for yourself instead of just working for someone else. Heck, if we thought anybody would wind up in your shoes, it would have been Sid." And didn't you bet Sid a hundred bucks that you'd be driving a Ferrari before your 30th birthday? Charlie's good-natured slam at his business partner's lackluster GPA and minimal motivation in college broke the tension

"Hey, hey, hey," Sid countered. "I'll have you know that what I lacked in grade points, I made up for in charm, and we never really shook on that bet." We all laughed.

Everything Charlie had said was true, and it was like a sucker punch to the gut. Though I had been discouraged when the big New York offers didn't come through, but I had gotten over it, accepted the position with Huntington, and went at it with all the intention in the world of making a name for myself there before moving on to what would surely be bigger and better and more fulfilling opportunities. When I left to join B + L, again it was in pursuit of finding a company that better aligned with my perspective as it related to running an effective and dynamic sales force.

"Tell you what, guys," I began to beg out, "I'm going to get some air. How about Jenny and I take a stroll around campus, and we all meet back for drinks and dinner at Canneloni's at 6:30?"

The Tenement Crew was all on board with my suggestion for dinner. Canneloni's was one of the nicest restaurants in town and always took good care of us when our crew visited. I always thought it was because Don probably slipped the maître'd a generous tip, but I could never be sure.

I took my leave immediately, grabbing Jenny's hand as we waved goodbye. "I had to get out of there," I told Jenny as soon as we were outside. "It was a bad as I imagined—airing my desperate life in front of the overachievers."

"David, Charlie didn't mean anything by what he said. Neither did Sid or any of the other guys. They were just referring to your reputation in college, you know. Everyone considered you the 'go-to' guy every time there was a group project assigned or something to be handled. Everybody knew, with you on their team, you'd take charge, and everybody would get a good grade. That's all they meant. Really…these guys are your oldest and best friends. They're not blaming you for this situation at work."

"I know, but everything Charlie said was the God-awful truth. Everything."

I stopped in my tracks and turned to face Jenny, looking her squarely in the eyes. "I'm going to go for a walk, by myself, if you don't mind. I've got to clear my head and get my mind around what is happening to me and what it means for *us*."

shift

"Sure, honey. Do whatever is best for you. I'll see you back at the hotel before dinner."

I leaned in to give Jenny a weak kiss and headed the opposite direction, back towards campus. I'd barely taken ten steps before I was overcome with the reality that was possibly—no probably—facing me. I'd handled things at the office in front of my team and tried to remain calm when sharing the news with Jenny; I'd even put up a good face in front of my oldest and closest friends. But now, away from it all, alone with my thoughts, the full force and far-reaching consequences of what could happen was almost paralyzing—and suffocating. I braced myself against a storefront to keep from falling to my knees and bringing further attention to my failures.

How did I end up *here*?

When did I sell out my soul for a company that's not even going to be around by the time I need to retire?

I don't even have enough passion left to make a single sales call, much less get out there and beat the bushes for 'the big one.'

I didn't know what was going to change, but I knew I couldn't keep going on like this. If the buyout didn't come through *this time*, it was just a matter of time before it happened again and I'd be right back in this same situation. I absolutely could not through this again. Every worst-case scenario I had imagined on the trip up here came rushing back. And even a few I hadn't considered.

I managed to catch my breath and steady myself before going on. For the next hour-and-half, I retraced the old haunts from my days on campus. Every campus landmark brought back a flood of memories—my freshman dorm and the pranks we all pulled on one another; the dining hall that was completed the year I graduated, and the bronze statue of the school's founder at the far end of the commons—a big, open green space where I used to play Frisbee with the guys, trying to impress the girls who were sunbathing.

I ended up at the student center where I saw a bunch of kids laughing and horsing around with one another, oblivious to the rude awakening that was awaiting them once they crossed the stage. Naïve kids. Just wait—wait 'til some faceless, thankless corporation sucks the ever-living life out of you and then tosses you aside for somebody younger and cheaper. I know you're thinking 'it won't happen to me.' Well, kids, I have got news for you—you don't even have a clue about the disaster waiting for you in 20 years…not a clue.

I headed back to the room by 6:00 p.m. with plans to take a quick shower and change clothes before heading to Canneloni's when I heard the all-too-familiar buzz of an incoming text and almost didn't open it but worried it might be one of the girls needing something. As soon as I clicked 'open,' I regretted it.

"EMERGENCY MEETING BEGINNING AT 7:00 P.M. TONIGHT. BE PREPARED TO WORK THROUGH SUNDAY NIGHT. ATTENDANCE MANDATORY."

shift

"Are you kidding me?" I didn't even realize I was speaking out loud. "*Now*, there's an emergency meeting, starting *in an hour*, and they expect everyone to drop everything and just show up. I couldn't even get there by 7:00 if I left now and went 100 mph all the way home. I'm not even going to give them the satisfaction of responding."

I was just about to start the shower when Jenny spoke up, "Honey, you know I trust you to do what's right and what's best for us, but don't you think you should maybe consider going to this emergency meeting?" Her usual calm demeanor was beginning to crack; I could hear it in her voice.

"You can't just show up and act like you never got the text. How about I help gather everything up, and we can be on the road in no time. You grab your stuff, and I'll be packed in five minutes. I'll text the group and tell them we're heading home, that you've been called into an emergency meeting. You know they'll understand."

"Now you get it," I wanted to say. "Now you realize your husband is the ne'er-do-well of the group—the golden boy who flamed out and who may very well be unemployed before the end of the month; the one with all the potential, all the hope, all the hype, and all the ridiculously unrealistic plans."

Now you get it.

shift

Second chances do come your way. Like trains, they arrive and depart regularly. Recognizing the ones that matter is the trick.

—Jill A. Davis

chapter six

We hardly spoke a word on the drive home. Jenny suggested stopping at the nearest Chick-Fil-A, but I couldn't think about eating at the time. I was not thinking about her, but only my pitiful self. By the time I pulled into our driveway, it was almost 8:30 p.m. and I knew I didn't have the luxury to even get out of the car when I dropped her off.

I had used the drive back to get into warrior mode, forcing myself to stifle the worries and doubts away for the moment and instead focus on the matter at hand. I also did some considerable thinking about what my dad and granddad would have done in my situation. What kind of man would I be if I didn't at least try to keep the job I've got for now? Dad would have never given up at this point; neither would granddad. They would have manned-up, shown up, and done whatever they had to do to get through it. I knew what I had to do, and that was to give this pathetic last-ditch effort my best shot and then figure out what I wanted the next 20 years to look like. Heck, if Sid and Charlie could make a fortune lending money to desperate people, I ought to be able *to do something* to keep a roof over my family's head. I willed myself to get my head back in the game.

No sooner had I reached the office and joined my team in the conference room than Barry put my new-found resolve to the test. "Jericho, we received a last-minute request for a proposal from Enzo Sopraffina, the luxury leather goods manufacturer in Italy. Remember meeting one of their head guys at Fashion Week in New York last year? He was shopping then, but not quite ready to test the waters in the American marketplace."

Barry didn't believe in waiting for others to answer what he considered obvious questions. "My wife said his purses are one of the hottest status symbols out there these days. Hollywood A-listers and East Coast socialites have them or want them, but up until now, they've only been available in Europe. You can order them online, but with very limited availability. They're so hot right now that most of their products sell out within minutes of being posted—kind of like hot concert tickets. It's like everyone is all hyped up about their style and quality and craftsmanship and all those other buzzwords people use to describe ridiculously overpriced products. So now, these guys are riding the wave of lots of notoriety and they seem to think now is the time to start shopping distribution options in the US. I don't think I need to tell you an account this size and prestige could go a long way to shore up our books and prevent the takeover.

"Anyway, I called in a favor from one of my contacts who knows people at Enzo, and we scored an introduction. It looks like my timing was perfect. They are currently entertaining proposals from the big US players and have invited B + L to pitch for the US business. But here's the catch—we're late to the game because they want somebody to make the pitch *in person* next week. And they want a commitment to present and confirmation of our itinerary by Monday *at the latest.*

"So, here's what's going to happen—you and I are going to go to this factory, meet with the Italians, and bring home this account. You're leaving Monday morning, first thing. I've already got Maggie working on your arrangements. You'll get the lay of the land and find out everything you can about this company, what the head guy, Enzo, is like, what the company culture is like, and what it is that makes their leather goods so unique— is it really a quality factor or just some clever branding and marketing angle they've worked on. We'll weave your findings into my presentation—you know—the touchy-feely stuff. You've done this shtick million times over; *it's what you do.*"

The way Barry said, 'it's what you do' almost made it sound like a secondary trait, not the very thing I considered to be *the* essential component of making an excellent sales presentation.

"So, if I'm doing the background work..." I started to speak.

"I'll get there on Wednesday, get a good night's sleep, and be ready to roll on Thursday morning. You'll bring me up to speed on the way to the factory, and I'll go in and close the deal. We'll come back as heroes! Either that, or you'll need to tell your

shift

team to update their resumes." And on that uplifting note, he walked out, leaving my team and me in the lurch and charged with trying to make the near-impossible become a reality.

Barry had never been one to mince words, especially when it came to calls to action for those working under him, and this time was no exception. He had 'cried wolf' so many times since joining the company, always overemphasizing the urgency to raise sales figures and land new accounts, which now, when it actually mattered the most, his do-or-die plan fell mostly on battle-weary ears. I could see it on the faces of my reps around the conference table. They were tired and hopeless men and women, called in for another edition of "Save Your Job."

I couldn't blame them for their blank stares. Like me, most of them had the battle scars of working under Barry for several years. The defeatist atmosphere Barry created had taken its toll on my weary soldiers.

I had to do something quick before the whole situation became hopeless. I knocked loudly on the long wooden table to gather everyone's attention. "Listen, I know, as things stand, the outlook is pretty dismal. I know most of you have been in this situation before—we get all riled up and start worrying about how we're going to make our rent or our car payment or whatever else expenses we all have, and then it fizzles out."

I took a deep breath and read the room for a moment. "But, this time...this time, I think this takeover could really go through if..." I was interrupted by the spontaneous chatter that broke out across the room as everyone started sharing their worries simultaneously.

"IF…," I tried to project above the noise, "if we don't do everything we can to land this Enzo account. Now, I don't say that as a threat, it's just a reality. All we can do is all we can do, and that is what I'm asking of you for the rest of the night and into tomorrow until we get this proposal as good as it can be." A few of the veterans gave me a nod of acceptance which I took as approval to continue.

"I commit to giving my best to doing the local background research once I get there and I have complete confidence that Barry will knock it out of the park when he presents." I had seen Barry step back in a few moments earlier. I also caught sight of his chest puffing out at the mention of his name.

"And then, however this all shakes out, we'll all have the comfort of knowing we couldn't have done more or done it any better. And we might just end up with some good 'war stories' about the weekend we saved B + L."

Most of my team seemed somewhat comforted by my off-the-cuff pep talk. Their posture had relaxed, and their expressions seemed to soften. If nothing else, I think it was of some comfort knowing their task-at-hand was finite and not some endless rabbit trail of possibilities as had occasionally been the case in the past.

Their charge was to give it their all until the 5:00 p.m. deadline Sunday afternoon. After that, they knew the pressure was ultimately on Barry and me to carry it the rest of the way. I needed them to hear the threat was real, but I also wanted to reassure them that their best efforts were all that was required of them.

shift

I could tell Barry noticed the shift in the mood too, though he would never have admitted it. "Way to steal my thunder, Jericho," he said in a hushed tone. "I was just about to light a fire under their lazy asses, and then you step in and tell them not to worry. That it's all on *me!* Just make sure, if this deal falls through, they know it's you to blame if they're out job hunting next month."

shift

Every human has four endowments -
self awareness, conscience, independent
will and creative imagination.
These give us the ultimate human
freedom... The power to choose,
to respond, to change.

–Steven Covey

chapter seven

The standard issue B + L proposal was long on facts, figures, and everything B + L could do for a customer. It was a longstanding, pre-set presentation template all sales reps were required to follow with little allowance for adjustments. It was also heavy on hype and lean on the relational aspect, something I remembered to be a priority after my brief conversation with the Enzo rep last year.

The one-size-fits-all pitch was just a formality for many of the long-standing B + L clients, especially those who were considered old school and actually could be courted with a case of single malt whiskey now and then. But it was clients like these that had ultimately been the reason for the declining market share and significantly reduced profit margin for B + L. Though still a contender in the distribution industry, B + L's image had begun to tarnish in the last decade due to the diminished prestige labels we once represented.

shift

After losing four major accounts in as many years, our reputation as the go-to distributor for ultra-high-end women's accessories had taken a severe hit. To compensate, company leaders directed their regional managers to refocus their efforts on lesser quality products, frequently courting the one-off lines of social media influencers and power bloggers who were hot for the moment. The downside was that these ultra-trendy designs only attracted a fraction of the market we once enjoyed with the longstanding and well-respected brands we once represented. In the short-term, some of the teams were able to make up for the decreased profit margin of the luxury products with an increase in volume by distributing to second and even third-tier retailers. Industry insiders had considered our concession a fatal mistake.

I did too, but my objections fell on deaf ears *again*.

As a result, at the time, I saw no other option than to play by the rules of those who signed my paychecks.

And yet somehow, one of the most sought-after brands in all of Europe was giving us the opportunity for an in-person proposal pitch, and I was tagged to do the research, backstory, and prep for the presentation within a couple of days. A million thoughts were racing through my mind. Maybe my persistence really had paid off. Perhaps this is the opportunity to break free from the by-the-book format. Maybe this is the door I have been waiting to open. Perhaps this is all a set-up, and I'm the sacrificial lamb for the company—the one who gets assigned the impossible client and who can be blamed for the demise of the company.

I knew a client like Enzo came around maybe once every decade and I was determined to put a unique and highly personalized proposal in front of them. Why not? It could be my swan song at B + L.

I had studied the Enzo website not long after meeting their representative at Fashion Week a few years ago. I don't know why I was so intrigued after only a brief meeting, but something about the guy just struck me as genuine. I remember him saying something about "when the time is right" and not being in any big rush to join the American retail scene.

Their website stood out too. So many of my clients' websites were just too crowded—trying to send a lot of messages or hit too many different markets with too much type, mediocre pictures, and lots of hype and over exaggeration about their products. Enzo's was different. Clean. Simple. Almost pure. The pictures were breathtaking and showed their products set amidst the gorgeous Italian countryside. Their copy was peppered with words like 'craftsmanship,' 'relationships,' and 'integrity.' I remember thinking to myself, "This is how to run a business."

I did a quick check of the current Enzo website and found it had remained much as I remembered it from last year. The pictures had been updated with the current line, but much of the brief copy remained the same. Again, the emphasis was on 'relationships' and 'integrity" and confirmed everything I suspected about the company: the usual B + L plan was in no way the best fit for persuading the Enzo group to do business with my company.

shift

I had just sketched a quick outline for my team based upon what *I thought* the proposal should emphasize and deleting what *I considered* unnecessary. No sooner had I made a few preliminary assignments than Barry stepped back in the doorway and hijacked my plans. "What the hell are you doing, Jericho? We do what works around here, and the template we've always used has always worked."

"Except when it didn't," I thought.

Barry almost physically pushed me aside, taking over my personal space to the point where I had to step back. "Listen up, folks, we're going to do what had worked for clients since before we all came here and will undoubtedly still work for them when we're long gone and that's sticking to our standard proposal template. This isn't rocket science people; it's what you've been trained to do."

And just like that, Barry was back in the thick of it, demanding sales forecasts, seasonal spreadsheets, and all the usual pieces of what he considered to be the Holy Grail of proposals.

My reps took turns casting questioning glances at me, looking for an indication for whose direction they were to follow—mine or Barry's. Fortunately, I could see the confusion that was about to go down and jumped in before Barry even knew something was up.

I took my turn to address the room. "Let's reset team. We need to have one voice, and we'll go with whatever Barry wants. He's doing what is best for all of us. Let's get those reports pulled together and consolidated so we can meet the 5-o'clock deadline and make it home in time for dinner with our families on Sunday."

I could hardly contain the resentment in my voice and hoped Barry wouldn't sense it in my tone. I certainly didn't believe a word of what I'd just said and didn't think many of my team did either. But what choice did any of us have at the moment?

Then I remembered my resolve when I first walked into the conference room—the commitment to give it my all and possibly, no probably, finish as strong as possible. I'd do as I was told to the best of my ability and leave it at that. If we didn't win the Enzo account, I knew the consolation wouldn't cover my outstanding bills, but I also knew I could live with myself a whole lot easier for having done so.

With 15 minutes to spare, my B + L team completed the official proposal and my admin, Maggie, sent the confirmation to Enzo, officially accepting their request for a proposal. She also sent word to Enzo headquarters informing them who would be representing B + L and our anticipated travel schedules—with me arriving late Monday night and Barry arriving Wednesday to make the presentation on Thursday. At Barry's direction, she had used the time while the sales reps were prepping to make travel arrangements for us.

Per the original request for proposal notes from Enzo, she booked me the first night near the Malpensa Express Milano Centrale terminal, the central depot for the train into the city from Malpensa International. A driver was to meet me the following morning and take me the 90-odd kilometers to the Enzo offices. Once in the region, Barry and I were booked at the Hotel Piccinelli, a significant step down from the types of hotels Barry preferred to stay at, but the nicest accommodations with availability near the Enzo headquarters.

The few times I had traveled with Barry, it was always an adventure. He always demanded to stay at the nicest place available whenever he traveled, often explaining his hefty expense account to accounting by arguing, "If we stay at a cheap place, it makes us look weak and unsuccessful. You don't want a client finding out we can't afford to stay in a nice place, do you?"

She booked me on a 6 a.m. flight out of Dallas with a layover at La Guardia before continuing to Milan. "I'm sorry for the early flight," Maggie offered. "It was the only one available with less than a day's notice. And actually, we were fortunate to get this flight. All the other, later options were full."

It would be a beating of a day—having to be at the airport by 4 a.m., a 3-hour layover in New York, and then an 8-hour flight to Milan. Add in the 7-hour time difference, and it would be 2 a.m. the next day on my body clock before I touched down in Italy. "Finish strong," I kept repeating. "Finish strong."

"Hey, you gotta do what you gotta do," I reassured her as I took the itinerary and boarding passes from her and headed towards the door.

Back at home, I came in the back door to see Jenny finishing up the dishes. "We had an early dinner tonight since I didn't know when you'd be home. Can I make you a sandwich or something?"

I should have been hungry by then but hadn't had much of an appetite since arriving back at the office Saturday evening. I had taken a few bites of cold pizza somebody had ordered a few hours earlier, but the rest of the time, I was getting by on coffee and adrenaline. I had been living off a steady diet of anxiety and fear since Jenny and I had driven away from the reunion yesterday.

"Nah, I'll get something at the airport in a few hours. I'm catching the 6 a.m. to New York and then on to Milan. Have to be at D/FW at 4 a.m., but don't worry, I'll grab an Uber."

"Oh honey, you've got to eat something, and you've got to sleep sometime. Doesn't Barry realize you've been up since Saturday morning and have hardly eaten since then, too? I'll make you sandwich and a fruit salad and…"

"I said I don't want anything!" I shouted. I knew she meant well, but I was beyond accepting another single order…from anyone…*even for a well-meaning sandwich.* I took a deep breath and tried my best to measure my words. "Look, I just need to get my clothes together, find my passport, and hopefully sleep a few hours before I have to be up again. Can I just take care of what I've got to take care of, please? If I want a sandwich, you'll be the first to know. I promise."

Jenny stood there speechless. I really did feel bad about my outburst, but I just didn't have it in me to talk through the whole apology bit at the moment. I thought it best to cut my losses rather than possibly make a bad situation worse. I turned and headed towards the hall closet to grab a suitcase and then onto

shift

our bedroom to throw a few things in a bag before a quick shave and shower and a hopeful 6-hours-worth of sleep.

The steam from the shower seemed to unknot every aching muscle in my body—at least for the short-term. Twice, while standing under the hot, hot water, I nearly dozed off; I was so exhausted. Once in bed, however, my mind kicked back into high gear as all the moving parts of this last-ditch effort came clearly back into focus. The minutes turned into hours as I tried not to consider all the things that could go wrong. I knew the chances of some element of this whole dog-and-pony-show not falling into place were staggering.

The more I thought, the more frantic I became, and the more sleep escaped me. Jenny had slid into bed beside me but hadn't uttered a word, preferring to lay on her side facing the wall. I checked the clock once more—12:30 a.m. "If I get to sleep now, I'll get 2-1/2 hours of sleep before I have to get up..."

It was the last thing I remembered before my phone alarm went off.

shift

Maybe every once in a while,
we can take a break from
doing everything faster and
quicker to reflect on who we
are and where we are going.

– Joe Plumeri

chapter eight

The flight from Dallas to New York was smooth and uneventful, and aside from the pilot's weak attempts at early morning humor and an overeager flight attendant offering coffee set-ups and off-brand biscotti, I was able to sleep a good part of the way. Exhaustion finally won out once I sat still and the interruptions were over. The physical and emotional toll of the last three days was almost too much to handle. Sleep was a welcome escape, even if it meant sitting upright at 30,000 feet.

I was startled awake when the pilot announced our approach to the city three hours later. It took me a few minutes to fully process where I was and what I was doing there. Had I imagined everything from the last 72 hours? Was it all just some unimaginable bad dream? The chaos that had become my life since Friday morning was overwhelming, especially as the reality began to sink in. I took the cue to raise my seatback and

shift

buckle my seatbelt in preparation for landing and then started to rehash all that had unbelievably happened: In just over three days, I had been told my job and the company as I knew them were both on the verge of evaporating; I'd come face-to-face with the glaring comparison of college buddies that were well on their way to making something of themselves in the business world and enjoying tremendous financial success in the meantime; I had been publicly shamed by my boss in front of my team and forced to prepare what Barry termed a 'do or die' presentation, transferring the responsibility of my team's future employment, if not the future of the company, squarely on my shoulders, and to top it all off, I hadn't had a civil word with Jenny since leaving to travel halfway across the world. "Yep, that pretty much sums it up. My life sucks."

Fortunately, I only had carry-on bags, so I did not have to wait in the baggage area but did have to shuffle through the winding TSA line again and walk the better part of a mile to a different terminal because last-minute flights couldn't be arranged on the same airline. The whole process took a little bit more than an hour-and-half, but the walk did me good. It was the most exercise I'd gotten since last week if you didn't count the pacing in the conference room.

I also realized I was hungry now— famished. I couldn't even remember when my last 'real' meal was. Thursday, maybe? The burger place directly across from my new gate looked adequate, and a burger sounded good even as early as it was. I was especially grateful when the hostess showed me to a small, but quiet corner booth near the back. When I opened the menu, my eyes landed on the picture of a glossy, mile-high burger. It'd been a long time since I'd indulged in a burger and fries, especially since Jenny had gone back to working part-time and became more interested in making healthier meals for the girls, as they had gotten older. She had even jumped on the Whole30 bandwagon like so many of her friends had and just recently, tried to pass off what she called 'zoodles' in place of real pasta. "Isn't it a great substitute?" she had asked. "They're zucchini strips cut to look like noodles. Get it? Zooooodles!" I pushed through the meal and feigned appreciation for her efforts but later made it back to the kitchen for a bowl of ice cream before going to bed.

As I ordered a bacon cheeseburger with fries and a cherry Coke, I couldn't help but think, "Maybe a heart attack will get me, and I won't have to deal with any of this." And that's when it hit me—I was considering a heart attack a good out to avoid facing my problems.

Before my meal arrived, I was able to set up shop with my laptop and settle in for the hour before my flight began boarding. When I looked around and noticed each of the tables was outfitted with a charging station for electronics, I couldn't help but think somebody at the burger place 'gets it.' Besides providing a meal, they also provided precisely what their customers wanted and needed. Genius.

The team at Enzo had requested information regarding who the presenters were to be and our flight plans. They also requested a digital copy of our proposal to be sent in advance of our arrival. This was my last chance to review the document we had prepared late Sunday afternoon before hitting 'send.'

As soon as I pulled up the document, my crosswords with Jenny the night before crept to the forefront of my mind. I really wanted to call and apologize but didn't think I had time to review the proposal one more time *and* get into a full-blown apology with Jenny. I knew it wouldn't be a quick phone call back home, so instead, I sent her a brief text promising to text when I landed in Milan and asked for forgiveness properly once I returned home. I was worried she'd consider it a cop-out, but more than anything, I honestly just wanted to seriously think things through on the long flight over and choose my words carefully. I wanted to apologize *and* explain my irrational outburst when all she had done was offer me a sandwich. I wanted desperately to assure her it wasn't her, but the chaos at work—the straw that broke the camel's—or rather, *my back*—under the extraordinary pressure.

Jenny responded with the heart emoji and told me she was praying for me and looked forward to hearing from me when I landed, and talk face-to-face when I returned. I was relieved to hear back from her so soon and felt like I had quite literally bought myself some time to make a proper apology.

When my order arrived, I shut down my laptop to give the burger my full attention as well as prevent an accidental spill on my computer. It had happened at one time or another to just about everyone in the office, but now was definitely not the time to take that chance.   Even though the burger was nothing exceptional, it was the best thing I'd had in a long time. Never mind that I swear I could hear my arteries clogging up with each bite, I savored every mouthful and then piled high the ketchup on the mountain of fries that came with it. Hoping for an expense account tip, the waitress kept the refills coming on my cherry Coke and asked for my dessert order as she cleared the table.

"You didn't like any of that, did you?" she smiled as she picked up my cleared plate.

"No ma'am," I chuckled. "I haven't had a meal like that in a long time—too long! But I can't squeeze in dessert after all that. Say, it doesn't look like your section is too busy right now. Would it be okay if I got some work done here for a while? My plane boards in about 30 minutes."

"Take your time, sir. We won't get another rush 'til lunch, and I'll be gone by then. Let me know if you need anything, and I'll wait to close out your tab in case you change your mind about dessert or want something to take on the plane." And then she was gone.

I turned back to my laptop and began scrolling through the familiar sections and company doublespeak. Some of the tabs were so familiar; I could recite the better part of them from memory. It was all so unbelievably uninspiring. I didn't know why anyone would want to do business with us.

We weren't offering anything more or different or innovative than every one of our competitors. Just once, I'd like to give my ideas a test run with an account like this—with a company that seems to merit something more than a cookie-cutter cut sales pitch. I thought about a quote I'd heard from Zig Ziglar years ago that seemed more relevant than ever. He used to say, "You will get all you want in life if you help enough other people get what they want." I knew that to the hard-core salesmen of Barry's generation, this way of thinking seemed counterintuitive, but I had never forgotten it and just once, I wanted to give it a try.

If it was up to me, I began thinking; I'd tailor every proposal to that client's unique needs and wants. I'd tap into their hopes for their product line and ask them what matters most to them. Was it always bottom-line driven? Or was maintaining brand quality a higher priority? Did they want a broad and diverse range of product offerings or did they want to focus all their efforts towards excellence with a smaller, more curated product line? What could we, as a distribution team, do for them to help reach their company's goals? I had never gotten on board with Barry's practice to make our presentations all about us, and not them. Whenever I put myself in our clients' shoes, I knew I would have desired a distributor to *show* me they were genuinely interested in my success, not give me all the hype about their company.

I literally could not stop the stream of consciousness flooding through my mind. One thought led to another and another until I decided to put my ideas down and draft my own 'Jericho world' proposal for my own satisfaction. I started out with the only thing I knew—the B + L standard proposal form, but when I was done, it held little resemblance to the company's unimaginative template. I deleted several sections I thought to be unnecessary and added a few more I thought were more relevant. I simplified the language, shortened the sentences, and listed question after question aimed at better understanding a client's priorities.

I added a paragraph about environmental issues to get a read on its importance to the client. I asked about their involvement in charitable organizations to get a better grip on their interests beyond business. I even suggested client representatives make a trip to Dallas so they could get an authentic taste of Texas culture and promised cowboy hats for everyone.

I had to laugh to myself as I typed as fast as I possibly could. Barry would think I had gone mad if he ever read a word of my ideas. I could seriously picture him doubled over laughing uncontrollably *before he called security to escort me out of the building.*

"One day, ol' boss…one day…" I thought as my fingers flew across the keyboard.

I had the official B + L proposal still open and saved and as 'Enzo,' so I was comfortable knowing I had the 'have-to' pitch ready to go. Besides, this perfect world dreaming was incredibly fun and motivating, and it sparked a creative side of me I hadn't indulged in for years. I named my new pitch 'Enzo 2.0' so that afterward, I could better compare mine versus theirs.

I was on a roll and would have kept going, but suddenly realized the final boarding call I heard was mine. I sprang into action—yanking plugs out, closing up documents, and gathered my things. And then I remembered—I had never sent the advance copy of the proposal to the people at Enzo.

shift

I couldn't believe I had spent all that time in my own little world, drafting an imaginary proposal no one would ever see. I flung open my laptop, begging the airport WIFI to connect.

"C'mon, c'mon, c'mon," I was begging for a connection.

Within a few seconds, the connection went through, and I rushed to write the world's shortest introductory email: "Looking forward to touring your factory, meeting your people, and learning more about the Enzo product line. Attached is our formal proposal to be presented by myself and Barry Nettles on Thursday morning at 9:00 a.m. Sincerely, David Jericho."

I was just about to hit send when I remembered to add the attachment. In the meantime, I peeled off two $20 bills and handed it to the waitress. "That enough?" I quickly asked. I didn't have time to even glance at my tab but knew New York airport restaurants were notoriously expensive.

"Yes, sir. Thank you very much," she nodded while calculating the $20 tip in her head.

I launched my email app, dragged the Enzo file in and hit the send icon as fast as I could, anxiously waiting to hear the swoosh of a successfully sent email. As soon as I heard it, I grabbed all my belongings and *raced* to board my flight.

"Last call for American Airlines Flight 754, nonstop to Milan, Italy, Gate 43. Again, this is the final boarding call for all passengers on Flight 754 to Milan, Gate 43. The door will be closing in five minutes."

I raced to the ticket and presented my boarding pass and passport. "You like to cut it close, don't you Mr…Mr. Jericho?"

"More than you know, ma'am," I managed to get out breathlessly. "More than you know."

"Welcome aboard American Airlines. I'm happy to inform you that you've been upgraded to Business Class due to our overbooking Coach seats. Enjoy!"

Finally…something going my way…or so I thought.

shift

It's not that I'm so smart,
it's just that I stay with
problems longer.

– Albert Einstein

chapter nine

It was evident which passengers had turned their phones to Airplane Mode and which had not on the long-haul flight to Milan. As soon as the plane got within cell service of Malpensa International Airport, the ding of incoming texts and emails of the noncompliant, such as myself, could be heard throughout the plane.

The first text was from Jenny, just after I'd had taken off from New York:

"My car is dead —not even turning over; called the repair place. Probably ignition. $800-$1,000 to fix. Where is your extra set of keys to the company car? Need something to drive until you get home."

"Well, that's just stellar news," I thought. "I'm probably going to lose my company car within a month, and the one car

shift

we do have needs some major repairs. When it rains, it pours, I guess." I texted Jenny back the location of the spare set of keys, top drawer of my nightstand, and was grateful I didn't have to address the car repair immediately. One more crisis kicked down the road a bit.

The other text was from Barry. He had traveled to New York on a separate flight to work the cocktail parties of Fashion Week and to attend last-minute strategy meetings with the company VPs before planning to fly out on Wednesday:

"A Nor'easter is supposed to move into the area tonight and dump 18" of snow and ice over every major thoroughfare in the five-state area. Doubtful planes will be operational; be prepared to present solo. I'll update you as soon as I know more."

I could feel the color drain from my face as I waited in the customs line. "This is unbelievable. This is freakin' unbelievable. I might as well get on the flight heading back home and cut my losses." I was mumbling out loud *again*.

"Next."

"Signore. NEXT!"

The impatient customs agent was oblivious to the fact that my world was literally falling apart around me. Two stamps to my passport, a double-check of my picture against my stunned face, and the agent waved me on with a heartless, "Welcome to Milan," as he signaled the next passenger forward.

I rode the Malpensa Express from the airport into the heart of the city. From there, it was less than a 5-minute walk to the hotel. I laughed out loud as I approached the Excelsior Hotel

Gallia. Here, we are facing a total buyout, probable termination, and ol' Tom goes and books us into a five-star luxury hotel. I guess we're going out in style.

I had to admit though; the place was unbelievably impressive.

I was greeted by a bellman who took my suitcase and briefcase and escorted me to the front desk for check-in. Two signatures later and the surrender of my credit card number to keep on file, and the bellman stood ready to show me the way to the guest elevator.

No sooner did the doors open on my appointed floor, then the bellman reappeared to deliver me to my room. As he showed me the room's amenities, the excellent view, and the note indicating nightly turn-down service, he was clearly proud to be representing this beautiful property. It was as if it was his charge to meet my needs and exceed my expectations. I could think of plenty of US companies, B + L first among them, who could learn a few things from my committed bellman.

I was well past ready to call it a night but texted Jenny that I had arrived safely and reminded her I was looking forward to apologizing in person. Even though I still had a few things to do in preparation for the presentation, I had enough sense to know that after I took a hot shower, it would be futile to try and review any notes regarding Enzo. I knew myself well enough to know I wouldn't have made it through the first few pages in my current state. My only viable option at this point was to get a full night's worth of solid, restful sleep and get at it full-steam ahead

shift

in the morning. Tomorrow was wide open other than meeting my designated driver and touring the factory. There would be plenty of time to polish the pitch and make adjustments after the tour. We'd done this same presentation hundreds of times before—this was old hat, *even if it was probably the last time I'd ever do it again.*

A few minutes later, I had the hottest shower I could stand and crawl between the elegant sheets. "I got this," I told myself as my head hit the pillow. "I got this."

shift

Nearly all the best things

that came to me in life

have been unexpected,

unplanned by me.

– Carl Sandburg

chapter ten

I felt like a new man after a full night's sleep and a respite from the mind-numbing weight of the responsibility I was feeling for so many people. I was also surprisingly more optimistic since I'd had a bit of time to process the news of Barry's cancellation. The old 'change what you can, accept what you can't' mantra had kicked in. What choice did I have anyway at this point?

I was also hungry. I checked my phone for messages and emails—nothing new from Barry, not surprising since it was just after midnight back home.

I was waiting to receive word from the Enzo people about my pick-up time and place but thought it best to be ready at a moment's notice. I dressed quickly and repacked the clothes I'd had on since I left home two days ago. Had it really only been two days since I left? The whole chain of events that had been set in motion since the news of B + L's doubtful future was *still* too much for me to process.

shift

Before I left for breakfast and checked out, I plugged my flash drive in to transfer the presentation. I planned to ask the concierge to make some printed copies during breakfast. Years and years of presentations had taught me that, no matter what, I always sent an advance digital copy of my presentation; clients always liked to have a paper copy in front of them during the pitch. I never really knew if it was because they hadn't taken the time to read the digital version or if they liked the sense of doing something like taking notes while I was speaking. Maybe it was the reassurance to have a hard copy in their hands. Whatever it was, I never presented a proposal without printed copies for all in attendance.

I also checked my itinerary one last time about the specifics of the day ahead—

"Company driver will meet you on Wednesday morning at 9 a.m. at the Cafe del Principe, near the Milano Centrale terminal, and take you to the factory for a tour; no prearranged time, just as you are able to get there. Check out of the Excelsior Hotel Gallia and bring your suitcase with you as you will be staying at Hotel Piccinelli on Wednesday night, much closer to the factory and corporate offices. The same driver will be at your disposal for further recon trips on Wednesday and will pick you up Thursday morning at 8:30 a.m. for the 9:00 presentation.

As soon as the presentation transfer was complete, I grabbed my suitcase and briefcase and rang for the elevator.

Once in the lobby, I stopped by the concierge desk, dropped off the flash drive, and requested ten collated copies be complete by the time I finished breakfast. Because I'd left my credit card on file, check-out was complete once I dropped my key off at the front desk.

Breakfast turned out to be quite an improvement over the traditional Continental breakfast most US hotels offered. The expansive buffet was both a feast for the eyes and a literal feast. After being seated, the waiter took my drink order and invited me to begin with the Italian pastries. "You may never get past them," he joked. "Many people are so taken by our beautiful bread and pastries; they never try anything else."

I worked to pace myself as I filled my plate, first with pastries and fruit, then eggs and thinly sliced meats. Knowing I had a long car ride ahead of me kept me from going all in and overindulging. Even still, I had more than I intended to and had to force myself to push my plate away. I had quit eating just to satisfy my hunger and was well into overdoing it just because everything tasted so good. For a brief moment, I even considered putting a couple of pastries into my briefcase but thought better of it when I realized how that might appear.

The copies were ready and waiting at the concierge's desk with a cover sheet and my name on top of the stack. I slid them into the outside pocket of my briefcase for easy access.

It was 8:50 a.m.—just enough time to walk to the café to meet my driver. Because the hotel was on a major thoroughfare and getting to the café involved crossing several lanes of traffic, I

shift

walked to the corner to cross at the light. I have to admit, though, the thought of taking my chances and racing through the traffic did briefly cross my mind as the life insurance payoff option still lingered in the back of my mind.

As I turned onto the side street where the café was located, I couldn't help but notice a bright yellow Ferrari parked front and center. In a row of small, nondescript European cars, it glistened in the sunshine. I had to pause to take it all in. The sleek and sexy profile, the louvered lines across the back window, and the unmistakable Ferrari stallion logo on the grill—all classic, all Ferrari, and all demanding to be admired. Here I was on the other side of the world, and I see the car of my dreams—a 1996 Ferrari 355 Spider—parked right outside my meeting place. I couldn't believe it. I considered taking a selfie right beside it and sending it back to the Tenement Crew, telling 'em I hit it big—landed the deal of the century! That would show them ol' Jericho still had a few surprises in him!

I decided against taking a selfie when I realized the owner was probably just a few feet away, possibly even inside the café, and watching my every move around his legendary car. "Be cool, Jericho. For God's sake, act like you've seen such an amazing automobile before," I told myself.

Inside the café, I surveyed the handful of people seated at tables and on couches. None of the customers appeared to be who I had imagined my driver to look like: it wasn't the group of three twenty-something young women chatting back and forth, taking turns showing one another pictures on their phones and laughing wildly, and it probably wasn't the matronly lady who was feeding tiny bites of her breakfast roll to the small dog at her feet; and there was little chance it was the sixty-ish man seated near the back who apparently had more interest in reading the newspaper than in looking to meet anyone.

"I'll have a Caffè Macchiato, please," I ordered from the barista at the counter.

"Sí, signore," he replied and turned to prepare it. A minute later, he brought me a tiny cup of steaming, almost syrup-like, coffee to my table. "You like?" he asked happily as he set it before me.

"Well, it's not exactly a caramel macchiato, but I'll give it a try."

"It's our house special," he said proudly. "Please, try."

Fortunately, the cup was still very much steaming, so I could only take a tiny sip to satisfy the gentleman. "WOW! That's intense! And hot too." I thought I had scalded both my tongue and my throat in a single swallow.

"It is how we enjoy, how you say, the true flavor of the coffee bean."

"Well, the coffee flavor certainly comes through—loud and clear! I think I just cleared my sinuses," I managed to say.

I was just about to ask him about my driver, but he had already turned and was greeting and hugging new patrons—townspeople who appeared to be regulars to the café. Instead, I bent over to reach into one of the outer pockets of my briefcase, hoping to find some long-forgotten gum that had maybe settled to the bottom. Just as I did so, a pair of well-worn men's shoes came into view.

"Scusa," an older man asked, "Are you, Signore David Jericho?"

Immediately, I straightened up, and in my rush to stand and extend my hand, I knocked the woven café chair backward. "Yes, yes I am. Are you my driver?"

"I am Saggio. And it would be my pleasure to take you where you need to go. It is the Enzo factory, no?"

"Yes! That's exactly where I need to go."

"Shall we?" Saggio asked as he motioned toward the door.

I reached for my suitcase and briefcase and followed Saggio out of the café. When he stopped in front of the Ferrari, I thought it was to admire it just as I had and expected him to keep walking towards the larger sedan parked beside it. When I started towards the sedan, he quickly corrected me.

"No, no…*this* is my car," he said still in front of the Ferrari. "molto bella."

"This…*this is your car? My driver* is driving a 1996 Ferrari Spider? I think I need to get a job driving people around Italy," I couldn't help but show my surprise and we both laughed.

In the meantime, Saggio had taken my small suitcase and briefcase from me and had opened the trunk which I remembered to be located in the front.

"The trunk is not meant for accommodating…" he began.

"Very much at all," I said, finishing his sentence.

"Correct. However, I think we will be able to squeeze these

two small bags in if I turn the larger one like this," he said as he worked to fit both of my small bags into the tiny space.

"Do you mind me asking how you were able to come by such a beautiful car?" I had to know, but I was also careful not ask how he *afforded* it, thinking there had to be some *other* reasonable explanation about how a 60-something chauffeur came into a piece of art like this.

"In time, my friend," Saggio replied. "Tell me a little about yourself first, please. "Is this your first time in Italy? Too bad you didn't bring your family. You are married, si?" And your flight, I trust it was acceptable?"

"Well, I am married and have been for going on 22 years. Her name is Jenny, and I gotta tell you, she puts up with a lot from me," I said with a grimace, thinking of how I left things with her the day before. "We're college sweethearts and have two daughters—Lauren and Suzanne. Lauren is a sophomore in college and Suzanne is a senior in high school, which means this time next year, I'll have two kids in college as well as an ailing father-in-law who is going to need some serious financial assistance in the next few years, too. And I'm facing the collapse of my entire..." I trailed off when I realized I'd only known this poor fellow five whole minutes and here I was dumping all the worries of the world on him.

"Sorry," I explained, "I didn't mean to get into all my personal problems so quickly. Just suffice it to say, the last 48 hours have probably been the most challenging of my life, but hey, what are you gonna do? I'm in Italy, in the car of my dreams,

shift

and all I can do is give it my all for what will probably be my last presentation with my current company.

"So *now,* tell me about how you came to own this classic piece of automotive wonder," I pressed for an explanation.

"I am glad you appreciate the car," Saggio began. "It is special to me as well. Perhaps if time allows, you can drive it before you return home."

I felt my eyes grow wide. "Are you serious? You'd trust me behind the wheel? Heck, I don't even know if I'd trust myself!"

"I will make sure we are out of harm's way—for us and others—and allow you to feel the power of the tremendous engine it has. But I must warn you— you will want one more than ever after you have driven it."

"No doubt about that! I have wanted one since I was a teenager, but a there's an awful lot of things that will have to change if that is ever going to become an option in my life. But believe me, just riding in it will be an unbelievable thrill. Have you had it a long time?"

"I have had it for the last ten years of my life. And like you, I had wanted one for a very long time, but I put off getting it for many years—too many. I always hoped to have one, but I kept waiting…waiting for what I wasn't sure. Eventually, I realized that if I wanted to be young enough to enjoy it fully, I needed to act. By then, I had already waited much too long—it is probably my greatest regret—putting off things that bring me joy and dismissing those that don't. I am reminded of this every time I drive it and grateful that I acted when I did.

"And, too, this is the most beautiful place in all the world—the vineyards, the villages, the countryside. These cars were made for these winding roads, and nothing but rows of century-old grapevines on either side of you. There are few things better than a drive through the vineyards near harvest time when the branches are heavy with grapes about to burst. It makes me very happy to share the experience with others. You must return in the autumn when the grapes are harvested. But until then, perhaps we can arrange a sunset drive before you leave."

"I would like that very much," I replied, but was quick to qualify my limited availability and pressing responsibilities. "That's assuming I get to the factory today for a tour and have sufficient time to review my notes one last time."

"Ah, yes. I understand. You have many things on your mind currently. But I must encourage you to relax during your time here and enjoy the simple lifestyle of our land. It is what adds the value to our lives."

"Are you always this introspective?"

"Well, Signore Jericho, my many years have taught me much—the good, the bad, the lean, and the prosperous times—they have all brought with them lessons that have helped me become the man I am today. I wasn't always so willing to learn, but my father taught me, as his father taught him, and his before that, that we are to savor the very moment at hand. That is because, there are always changes and challenges and opportunities coming at us—some are significant, some are not, but either way, they shape our lives. He helped me to see and

shift

understand these shifts for what they truly are—turning points with much to teach us. I used to think it was babble coming from an old man; now I am the babbling old man." We laughed again.

I couldn't quite put my finger on what it was exactly, but I was definitely intrigued by my driver—both by the surprise of him as my driver with his own Ferrari as well as by his insight. Admittedly, he had done more than just drive people around all his life.

Intrigue aside, I was still consumed with all that had been put upon me in the last 48 hours. I lost myself in thoughts as Saggio took me to the city's highways leading out of town. Within a few minutes, the city was behind us, and I was wholly engrossed in the shortcomings of my life at this point. I forced myself to take a hard look at where I was in life *right now*, where I was headed, and even paused to contemplate if I had learned anything from the shifts that had occurred *and were still occurring* at a staggering rate in my life.

Saggio had made it seem so simplistic: face a few challenges, suffer a setback now and then, learn a lesson or two, and move on. Maybe that's how it works in a tiny Italian village, but not so much in a major US city. It was never that simple.

I went back and forth between feeling convicted by Saggio's words and justifying the dismal state of my life due to things beyond my control. What's done is done, I reasoned. I'd given up on all those 'dream it and do it' perfect world ideas. I was just trying to keep my head above water and make it through all that was coming at me *now*.

I was so lost in my thoughts I didn't even realize Saggio had asked me a question. "I'm sorry—could you repeat that?"

"No problem at all, friend," Saggio replied. "I asked about your plans for this trip. What are you hoping to accomplish?"

"I am coming to tour the Enzo factory and present a proposal for them to do business with my company back in America. My company is on the verge of being bought by another, bigger company and unless I win this account, we have no chance of fighting the takeover and lots of people will likely lose their jobs, including me. Originally, I was to come here and get a look at the factory, learn about their processes and manufacturing capabilities and then incorporate that into our presentation. The plan was for my boss to fly in tomorrow, have me bring him up to speed on everything, and then he'd go in and close the deal. But, I just got word yesterday that he's snowed-in in New York and can't catch a plane out of there in time for our meeting on Thursday.

"Sorry Saggio, I know I sound so defeated. I'm just overwhelmed with the responsibility I feel to save so many people. If they only knew I'm not even doing a good job of saving myself, I think they would have realized they were better off sending someone else. But apparently, what I sent last time to the head honcho there must have struck a chord because we almost won the account then and now they're asking for another, different pitch. Tell me, do you know this Enzo character? Is it Mr. Enzo or does he just go by Enzo? I'm not even sure how to address him."

shift

"Oh, signore, *everyone* in this part of my country knows of Enzo—he is a good man."

"Really? How so?" Suddenly I realized my recon work had just begun.

"Enzo is everybody's friend, and everybody is his friend. He has benefited much from his company and works diligently to share his riches with others—sometimes it is money, sometimes it is gifts, and still other times it is through a word or two of encouragement when he shares tales from his life. He gives what he considers best for those in need.

"However, one thing you must know about Enzo—he prefers to live a simple life. He still plays bocce ball with the old men in his village most days because they were his friends—his true friends—before others came to think of him as the rich and powerful Enzo."

"Interesting. What does Mr. Enzo look like? I searched his company website, and there were no individual pictures of the company's top people—you know, like pictures of the important people with all their qualifications listed beside their picture."

"He prefers to get to know people outside of the factory, to see who they truly are, to come to understand their soul, their *anima*," Saggio said as he tapped his chest for emphasis. "That is why there are no personal pictures—because you cannot capture a person's soul in a photograph. You must get to know them, observe them in good times and bad, watch their interactions with others, and discover what is of value to them. Only when you come to learn these things can you really get to know someone well. He doesn't care for all the fuss that is made over his generosity to so many friends and family. In fact, he is known for saying, 'I'm just Enzo, from Parma, nothing more.'"

"So, you know him?"

"Oh, very well. I see him every day. That is how it is with Enzo. He values relationships above all of his business dealings because, as he says, that is where the joy of life is found. He makes it his goal to find the good in everyone he meets, though he'll be the first to tell you, sometimes that's like looking for a needle in a haystack!" We both chuckled at his irreverent reference to the difficult people in our own lives who came to mind.

"So, you can't give me at least a little description of what he looks like, then? I get the whole importance of getting to know who someone truly is; I'm just wanting to have a picture in my mind of who I'm going to meet this week."

Saggio hesitated a moment before responding. "He looks like me. Like my uncle. Like the man who runs my local market. He is an older Italian man who looks like all of us. Nothing remarkable, just like so many of us in our village."

I could tell I was getting nowhere. And again, Saggio broke my train of thought: "Signore Jericho, I see in you a man committed to doing his best for his company. It is clear you are carrying much responsibility for many."

I nodded in wholehearted agreement thinking, "You have no idea, Saggio…no idea at all."

And then he continued: "Yes, maybe you have encountered some serious challenges, and may even consider yourself to be in a hopeless situation, but I want to reassure you that you might also have the good fortune to learn, possibly even gain, from these difficulties. I have faced many trying times in my life too, but like me, you will eventually be able to move forward and accomplish much—even if your journey takes you on a few unexpected detours."

"I appreciate it, man," I answered, "but let me get through this 'pitch-of-the-century' and then we'll talk philosophy. Deal?" I hated to cut him off but knew he could never appreciate the level of trouble I was facing. Sure, his ideas worked *for him* and his minor league issues, but I was in the majors—facing major challenges and potentially devastating major consequences. "Save your pontificating for the next passenger," I thought.

Saggio took the cue and returned his focus on the road, and we traveled the next 10 minutes in silence. It wasn't until he became worried over a sound he heard coming from the engine that we spoke. As he downshifted, his expression became worried. When he pulled over to the side of the two-lane country road, I did my best to hide my rising anxiety level. "What are you doing?" I almost demanded.

"I hear something—a sound coming from the engine that is not right. I must check it out before we get too far down the road and away from those who can help us." Saggio jumped out and popped the hood open while the engine was still going. He leaned in to take a better listen before latching the hood back in place and returning to his driver's seat.

"Something isn't right," he said. "That sound is signaling trouble. I must take it now to my mechanic, Gianni—he is the best in the region."

"But, what about getting me to the factory?" I was growing more worried by the minute.

"Signore Jericho, I will get you where you need to be when you need to be there. Okay? We can even contact the factory when we get to Gianni's shop, and he can tell us what he must do to fix the car."

I nodded my acceptance again, wondering what choice I honestly had in the matter.

"Signore Jericho, I sense your frustration at the delay, but allow me the courtesy to explain, please."

Once again, I nodded.

"There was a time when I believed there was nothing I couldn't master, even to the point of repairing my car. However, I almost ruined the engine after one of these attempts and had since come to appreciate the value of other people's knowledge and insight and experience—especially on things I am not familiar with. I did not have the tools nor the knowledge when I first tried to fix my car. And I almost did irreparable damage to it. It was an expensive lesson that I have never forgotten.

"I cannot possibly know all there is to know about everything in my life, so I work to find those who do know what I don't and who put it into practice exceptionally well. That is how it is with Gianni, my mechanic. Ever since my disastrous attempt to fix the engine myself, I have trusted Gianni to handle everything as it relates to my cars. In turn, he has taught me what I must do to keep it in excellent running condition.

"Just as I know what I do and I do it well; Gianni knows what he does, and he does it very, very well. He couldn't do what I do, and I certainly couldn't do what he does. That is why I trust him with my car.

"In many ways, Gianni has helped me to maximize my performance—certainly concerning driving, and occasionally, in my life. He has taught me much about the inner workings of my car because he has spent his lifetime caring for these fine automobiles. He has become my consultant of sorts in that he provides a framework within which to service my car—when to check this sound out, when to bring it in for fine tuning, and many other simplistic processes that have sometimes seemed overwhelming…until I consider the cost of neglecting them. He has held me accountable for maintaining my responsibilities with the upkeep of the car through the years. I am a better driver because of Gianni's presence in my life.

"Like many young people, I had to experience several serious misfortunes before I came to value the wisdom and knowledge of others over and above mine in some areas. It took me a long time to realize and accept that seeking help is not a sign of weakness; it is a sign of strength! In time, I came to understand wise men seek advice and many advisors can bring success. The wisest men I have ever known are the ones who knew *when* to seek help and *where* to seek help. Now, I readily do the same."

I wasn't quite sure how to respond. Admittedly, I was again struck by his acute insight, but I was still also very much concerned with getting to the factory promptly as well. In another setting, without the pressures I was feeling, I would have welcomed Saggio's stories and tales of wisdom, but for now, I didn't have the luxury to indulge him.

"I gotta tell you, Saggio," I started, "I love hearing all you've got to say, but I've also got to get to the factory if I'm going to have any chance of saving my job and helping all those folks back home. So yeah, I'm good to stop by your mechanic's shop for a few minutes, but after that, we're really going to make up some time on the road. That work for you?"

"It will all work, Signore Jericho…for you, for me, for Enzo. Everything will work out."

shift

Plans go wrong for lack
of advice; many advisers
bring success.

— Proverbs 15:22 (New Living Translation)

chapter eleven

Five minutes after making a call to Gianni, Saggio exited the two-lane highway onto a smaller, more country road. In the distance, I could see the outline of two and three-story colorful buildings and the occasional one-story. Further on, Saggio turned onto yet a narrower road, a back-alley pathway of asphalt, apparently not a street like I was used to in the States. As he approached the main road leading into the village, it once again became slightly more solid, made entirely of pieced-together stones and mortar. It looked like a gigantic jigsaw puzzle put together with some serious craftsmanship.

Remarkably, the village closely resembled the image Hollywood had come to perpetuate in movies as the typical Italian landscape—flower boxes in full bloom hanging from two and three-story windows, laundry hung on lines between buildings, and children chasing one another in and around the stalls of the corner market. There were even old men playing bocce ball at the tiny park next to Gianni's shop. I wondered if they knew of Enzo too.

As soon we pulled to a stop, dozens of children surrounded the car, each chanting, "Papa, Papa, Papa!" and jumping up and down, stirring up the dirt driveway. "Whoa, Saggio, either you've been really busy and have some explaining to do, or everyone here thinks you're their Papa!"

Saggio laughed and reached behind the seat. Inside was a bag of multicolored candies—hundreds of dime-sized bits of sweetness, each individually wrapped. He reached in and began depositing three and four, sometimes five, into the waiting and open hands of the children. A chorus of "Grazie, Grazie, Grazie" came from the children as they received the candies and in turn, stepped back for those behind them. "Luca, Ti ho dato qualcosa in più da condividere con il tuo fratellino quando si sente meglio - devi condividere! Promettere?" He told me that Luca's little brother was sick and to be sure he took him some candy too!

The little boy was already turning to leave but turned back to nod and say "Promettere," to his benefactor.

Saggio turned his attention back to me to explain. "Years ago, when I came here, I had a large bag of candy with me. I don't even remember why I had it, but one of the children saw it and yelled for all the others to come and see it. That little bag of candy brought them such delight back then that now I rarely travel without a generous bag stowed away. I never know when

I will be here next, but whenever I come, I want to continue the legacy of bringing them tiny bits of happiness."

"You certainly know how to make a grand entrance, my friend," Gianni said as he grabbed Saggio by the shoulders and air-kissed each cheek before embracing his old friend. The two men laughed, and Saggio pulled away to introduce me.

Gianni didn't hesitate: "If you are a friend of this man, you are my friend too," he said as he pulled me into a hearty embrace.

"Well, thank you," I choked out after catching my breath from the wind that had been knocked out of me.

Saggio turned back to Gianni and began speaking in rapid-fire Italian, explaining the sound he'd heard and where it was coming from. At my request, he also mentioned I was on a short timeline with plans to tour the Enzo factory before the end of the day. Gianni assured Saggio he would look at it immediately and hopefully have us back on the road within the hour.

"Perfetto!" Saggio exclaimed as he translated for me. "We have just enough time for a cup of coffee and maybe a treat ourselves! Follow me."

Saggio took the lead and began walking down the main street of the village, stopping to visit with people on the street occasionally. Half a block down was the small café Saggio had selected. He greeted the owner as an old friend and immediately took the liberty of ordering for both of us. "You must try the espresso—it is the best of anywhere in Italy!" he said as the old woman behind the counter offered us each a cup.

shift

"You Italians like your coffee some kind of strong," I said as I took the tiniest sip possible from the cup.

"Si, si, we do. We like to grind the coffee as we need it to preserve the intensity of the bean. Then, when we grind it and press the very hot water through the grounds, it is as flavorful as it can be. We countrymen have a hard time understanding why so many Americans put syrups and whipped cream and all other sorts of nonsense on top of a perfectly good coffee. It seems such a waste to us."

"That's us! Good ol' Americans—always wanting to take something to the next level. Bigger, better, more indulgent. For better or worse, it's the American way," I explained.

Thirty minutes later, a young boy came running into the café. "Papa, Papa, Signore Gianni—he says your car is ready."

"Grazie," Saggio replied and reached into his pocket to give his loose change to the boy.

"Ahhh, Grazie, Papa!" the boy could hardly contain his pleasure.

As soon as we returned to the auto shop, Saggio was again surrounded by the local children hoping to score a second round of candy. He was quick to oblige the excited children and went to retrieve the candy from his car. The children fell in place behind him, following him toward the garage, like a modern-day pied piper.

I took the opportunity to step aside and ask Gianni if he was familiar with Enzo or had possibly even met him.

"Oh, si, signore!" he couldn't contain his joy at the mention of Enzo. "He changed my life! He helped me in ways I could never see for myself. Before, yes, I knew Ferrari's very well, but I was still just a local mechanic, meeting the needs of my townspeople. But when he trusted me with his valuable cars, people took notice. Everyone from around here and well beyond began coming to me with their beautiful cars."

"All because Enzo allowed you to work on his car?" It seemed like a giant leap from repairing old broken cars to regional fame.

"Oh, signore—there is so much more to it! By working on his cars, I became very familiar with the workings of the Ferrari engine. Underneath the beautiful exterior, it is a delicate piece of machinery; that is what enables the car to travel so fast and so smoothly. It must be maintained by someone who knows the inner workings intimately. It has taken me many years to become this proficient, but the reward has been so very worth it."

"What do you mean 'the reward?' The increased business? The notoriety? And what's the deal with everyone around here having a Ferrari? I mean Saggio has one, and now you're telling me Enzo has at least one, if not more."

"Ferraris are recognized as the premier car of Italy. It is the desire of many men from my country to own one sometime in his lifetime. That is why knowing how to best service and repair them has become such a valuable skill. I am one of very few who are considered master mechanics by the people from Ferrari. That means they know my level of expertise and officially endorse me. It has brought business from all over—more than I can ever handle by myself."

shift

"So, you're saying; you've got Ferrari's backing as the 'go-to' guy to fix their cars? And that there's very few of you who are authorized by Ferrari? So, what does that mean for some ol' schmuck in France or Spain or wherever who needs his car worked on? Does he have to ship it to one of you specialty guys?"

"That is the joy, signore! That is where the joy is! Ferrari owners know that to maintain the value of their cars, they must be serviced by the best. If someone uses an unrecognized mechanic, they risk losing a lot of value when they go to sell their car. I have worked with the team at Ferrari to create a program for the young people to learn the craft, to carry on the tradition of exceptional service for an exceptional car."

"You've developed an educational program, kind of like an internship? And Ferrari is backing all this?"

"Oh yes—they are backing it, they are supporting it, they are providing all the necessary tools for us older ones to pass on the knowledge we have gained through our many years of working on their cars. I have a waiting list of young men and women wanting to enter the program and apprentice under me as do the other master mechanics. We are teaching as fast as we can!

"That is because, after they complete the training here, Ferrari will set them up in auto repair shops across the world where there is a large concentration of their cars. They are helping to better serve their customers; we are equipping young men and women with a valuable and very marketable trade, and the legacy of the Ferrari name can continue into the next generation."

"All because of one man who let you work on his car…"

"All because of one man who invested in me," he corrected. "That is the difference."

About that time, Saggio returned to our conversation, having double and triple-dipped into the bag of candy. The children in the background were squealing with excitement as they compared their stashes. And Saggio…well, Saggio was beaming too. With nothing more than a bag of penny candy, he had brought an afternoon of happiness to nearly two dozen children.

Saggio reached for his wallet to pay Gianni, but Gianni would have none of it. The repair was on him today, he explained. My first thought was that he couldn't stay in business too long if he made this courtesy an everyday thing; my second thought was "Wow! He just dropped everything else he was working on to take care of us; he repaired a Ferrari in 30 minutes, and he said it was on the house." He was either a customer service guru or a fool for all he had done for us—and I wasn't sure which one at that point.

Gianni stepped forward to hug us both again gratefully and once again, I felt the air being squeezed from my chest. "Until next time, Signore Jericho," he said as he waved and we pulled out of his lot. "Until next time!"

"I had the most interesting conversation with Gianni," I started to explain to Saggio. "Do you know he is one of only a few master mechanics in the region authorized by Ferrari? That's pretty amazing by itself, but he's also teaching a whole new generation of kids his skills so that the practice can go on long after he's gone. He said he was just a local mechanic until Enzo helped transform his life. You don't hear too many of those 'rags-to-riches' stories anymore like that."

"He has done very well," Saggio said smiling. He just needed a bit of encouragement and some good advice from the outside to see his potential."

"I could use my own personal Enzo—you know, somebody to keep in your back pocket to encourage you when things go south." Before I knew it, I was daydreaming about how different my life would look now if I'd had someone step in and encourage me like Enzo had done for Gianni.

I snapped back to reality when I heard Saggio shift into fourth gear. There was not another car in sight, and the road belonged to us. Before I knew what was happening, we were going well over 200km/hr. I did the math in my head and shouted above the roar to Saggio, "Aren't we going over 120 mph?" He nodded in agreement without taking his eyes from the road. It was faster than I'd ever been in a car and it was exhilarating. Still, I clinched my door handle with all my strength.

The daydreaming could wait—especially if I didn't win the Enzo account. "So, on to the factory now?" I shouted.

As Saggio began downshifting, the roar of the engine started to die down. "Yes, but, I must treat you to lunch at my favorite spot in all the region."

"Saggio, really—I can skip lunch, eat later—whatever it takes. I have got to get to the factory!"

"Very well, Signore. If I promise to get you to the factory by later this afternoon, will you do me the favor of enjoying a very special lunch with me?"

"As long as you get me to the factory on time, I will eat your lunch, Saggio. Listen, it's not that I don't really appreciate your kindness, and I get wanting to share your country's specialties, but I've got a lot riding on this…Heck, I've got *everything* riding on this!"

"I will get you there when you need to be there—I give you my word," Saggio promised as he turned onto the main road.

For the next half-hour, Saggio drove at a leisurely pace, often allowing others to pass him as if he had no specific destination in mind. The laid-back pace began to grate on me to the point where I asked if he might consider picking up the speed a bit.

"If we speed through the beauty of the countryside, we will be poorer for it," was all he said. And all I could think of was how poor I'd *actually* be if I lost this account and my job. I wanted to put 'my poor' up against 'his poor' and see what he'd say then. I'll see your so-called poor from missing out on the countryside, and raise you a mortgage, college tuition, and an old folks' home. I was confident 'my poor' was considerably greater. However, I allowed discretion to prevail, and I held my remarks.

Along the way, Saggio pointed out what he considered to be the landmarks of his homeland. In reality, they were mostly personal spots that had come to mean something to him throughout the years, but still, it gave me a better understanding of the land and people that had shaped him. "That is my cousin's farm where I learned to milk goats when I was a boy," he said, pointing out a sizable field full of goats.

"And that…that is my great, great-grandmother's homeland. The house is not standing anymore, but it still holds so many family memories for me."

"And just past the hillside, see that white building? That is the school that my father built for orphans. These hills and fields and vineyards are rich with memories for me. Do you have such a place as this—a place filled with happy memories of your past, David?"

I had to think for a minute. "I guess you could say my college campus, probably. It's where I made some lifelong friends, met my wife, and thought I knew what I wanted to do with my life. Turns out, I was a foolish kid thinking I was going to change the world. Man, I was off-base."

"What do you mean—you were foolish? What does this 'off-base' phrase mean?"

"Off-base? It's a baseball term; it just means I was nowhere near to understanding how life really works. I had interned at a company the summer before graduation and high hopes of making a name for myself in New York City. I did the usual resume/interview gig with some of the big management houses in New York, but no one ever extended an offer. So, when my old company back home came through with a position, I thought I'd take it, bide my time, and *then* make my fortune after I had a little experience under my belt.

"Next thing I knew, I had a wife, a kid, another on the way, and a hefty mortgage. And I'd been at the company for seven years. I felt like my career, and the rest of my life had already been plotted out when I wasn't paying attention. At that point, I didn't feel like I could take my pregnant wife and a toddler away from everything they knew to land a job in the big city. I felt stuck by the time I turned 30."

"That is no way for someone so young to look at life," Saggio offered.

"Tell me about it," I commiserated. And then, so as not to sound completely ungrateful, I added, "I don't mean to make it sound like it's been all bad—it really hasn't. I love my wife, and I've got two terrific girls. I've made a decent living through the years, but not what you'd want to retire in grand style or anything like that. And my job? Well, it's a job. It covers our expenses with a little to spare. I've got a company car, so that's one less thing to worry about, and I've got a great team that works under me. I do what I do, come home, and go back the next day. Isn't that why they call it 'work'?

"And are you happy? Content?" Saggio asked.

"Well, yes and no," I answered truthfully. "When I see what the guys I graduated with are doing now, it's hard to believe we all started at the same time, had the same kind of background, and roughly the same opportunities…or so I thought. The funny thing is, I was the one everybody thought would rock the business world. Instead, I was the one that settled while they took all the chances and the risks. They either started companies or at least joined 'the right companies' back then. And now, let's just say they're all knocking it out of the ballpark with second homes, extravagant cars, and traveling whenever and wherever they want—basically living the life I thought I would be living by now."

I had to pause for a moment just to let everything I'd just said sink in, more for my sake than Saggio's. "And then…like I said earlier, last week, the wheels literally fell off my career and subsequently, my life."

"Signore Jericho, I am so sorry to hear of this. Is it really that dire?"

"Saggio, it is 'that dire' and then some. Like I said, if these venture capitalists are successful in buying out B + L, there will be duplicate people in virtually every position—two heads of HR, two EVPs over purchasing, two Midwest Sales Directors like myself. The company can't support such a doubling up of personnel and that almost always means the new folks on the block are the first to go. In this case, it would be the people at B + L."

"And so now all the responsibility rests with you now to win the Enzo business?"

"Every last bit of it…Every last bit of it."

Saggio waited a moment before asking, "Tell me—why don't you change where you are? How you are living. What you are doing."

"Well, let's see…there's this little matter of people depending on me to provide for them—both at work and at home. I can't just up and walk away from this train wreck…at least not yet. But, don't think I've haven't thought about it—many times over!"

And then, almost as an afterthought, I felt as if I needed to justify my current state of upheaval: "I remember in the early years, even though I had never made the leap to New York, I was still full of ideas, you know, ways to fix this problem or that, ideas for how to serve our clients better, in a more personalized way. I even rewrote the bible of our business—the hallowed B + L proposal template.

"Man, you'd have thought it was blasphemy the way the higher-ups shut me down; they even accused me of 'wanting to give the company away' when I suggested concentrating more on doing what was *really* right for the clients over the profit margin. They made it clear from that point forward that being a team player meant doing things their way. And so, in the interest of keeping my job, I thought it best to keep my ideas to myself."

"So, you never presented your ideas again after all these years?" Saggio was intrigued and wanted to know more.

"Oh, I still wrote up my own versions from time to time, but mostly just to entertain myself. It helped keep me sane and even got the ol' entrepreneurial juices flowing now and then."

"Let me see if I understand this dilemma you face," Saggio began. "You feel as if you are where you are because of others and the limitations they have put on you? And because you have a family, you have been unable to pursue a career that is meaningful to you? And because your company is unreceptive to your ideas, you are unable to service your clients as you think best? And lastly, you consider yourself a failure compared to your schoolmates? Am I correct?"

shift

It was stunning to hear my life spelled out in such an indicting manner. "Well, it sounds pretty pathetic when you put it like that."

"That is not the intention at all. I only wanted to see if I gathered the facts from your story correctly. I mean nothing but complete respect for you. Let me tell your story another way: I see a man deeply committed to providing for his family, carrying the burden of dependence at work as well, not just for those that report to him but for the future of the entire company. And I see a man who may not be where he intended to be at this point in his life, but that still has the potential to realize many of his unfulfilled plans—both personally and professionally."

"I gotta admit, I like that version much better."

"Remember what I said about the significant challenges of our lives—the transitions that affect us most deeply? Turmoil at work can often become turning points for each of us. What we do with them, how we react to them, what we do in the aftermath— that is what reveals a man's character.

"Even though it may not seem like it now, you have before you the potential to make tremendous decisions about your remaining days—what you want for you personally and as a man, what you want of your marriage, your family life, and yes, your career. This is true regardless of how the Enzo account and the future of your company turn out. Wouldn't you agree?"

"I get what you're saying...I really do, but there's just so much more to it than that—so many variables, so many people, so much *everything*. It's just nowhere near that simple."

"Ask yourself, David, what if it was?"

I put my head back against the headrest and closed my eyes. This conversation with my driver—*of all people!*—had gotten way too deep way too fast. Or had it? Saggio had done what I had chosen not to do after having known me only a few hours, and that was to strip away the excuses, the blame, and the justifications for where I was at this point in my life. It was a hard truth to face, and even harder to begin to accept, but I was fast coming to appreciate my random encounter with Saggio.

shift

*Life can only be
understood backwards;
but it must be
lived forwards.*

– Soren Kierkegaard

chapter twelve

The engine revs increased as Saggio downshifted to make the turn into the vineyard and I straightened up in my seat. All around us were precision-straight rows of grapevines, most of which that had been trimmed back since the harvest a few months prior. The rows went on as long and as far away as the eye could see. One look at the extraordinary fields, and it was apparent this was an extremely well cared for operation.

"This is my Aunt Sophia's family vineyard. It has been in our family for many generations—as far back as anyone has records. And now, her family and her children's families work to maintain the history of this soil," Saggio explained as we pulled up to what appeared to be a winery. "I need to get a special bottle of wine for our dinner tonight," he said. I didn't know if he was talking about dinner with other people or me later that evening.

shift

Either way, I stayed in my seat thinking he would be right back. That was not to be as he opened my door and waved me out. "Come, I will introduce you and show you around."

"I must have taken leave of every last sense I ever had," I thought, "to be out here touring a winery *with my driver* when I should be learning everything I need to know about Enzo."

Still, I just couldn't shake the brutally honest insights about my life that Saggio had shared with me just moments before. One thing was for sure: I had a lot of thinking ahead of me. I was still lost in thought but rushed to catch up with Saggio just as he was entering the huge metal building that was the warehouse.

Once inside, I saw more specialized machinery than I had ever seen in my life—tremendous, stainless steel industrial-sized vats, bottle sterilizers, label applicators and more—virtually everything that was necessary to transform fresh-picked grapes into wine. "As you say in America, this is where the magic happens," Saggio said with a broad-sweeping gesture across the entire operation.

"Wow! So this is how it's done. This is a pretty major operation here."

"Yes, it is. This region is known for producing some of the best Chianti in the world, and this vineyard, in particular, has played a significant role in bringing recognition and honor to the vineyards of this area. We are all very proud of the heritage of this land. It has served our family and the people of this area well for more than a hundred years. That is because we are careful to respect the heritage that has brought them to this point.

"We…they…we all have come to see that by honoring the rich, rich history of those who have come before us, we are able to benefit. By nurturing these vines and perfecting the process of turning grapes into excellent wine, my family is now able to produce world-class wines that are greatly valued."

"That's an admirable concept, but how do you make sure something isn't lost in translation, so to speak—you know, from the old folks to the younger, maybe more independent generation?"

"We begin when our children are little," Saggio explained. "We teach them to honor the past and invest in the future. We encourage them to study what we do and how we do it; to take inventory of what has worked and what could be improved upon. In doing so, they are able to learn from the successes and failures of those who have come before them and to whom they owe much gratitude. We want them to know that although you cannot change the past, you can use it to shape your future."

"You could teach a lesson or two on parenting to several people I know back home," I told him good-naturedly. "That 'honor' and 'respect' thing always seems to get pushed aside in favor of something 'cool and trendy.'"

"Signore, my word to you is to always learn from where you have been and what you have done. In doing so, you will always be better prepared for the future than if you ignore it. It is not always an easy task, but it is always of value."

"Good word. Now, how about that 'to die for lunch' you promised me?"

shift

After a longer-than-expected tour of the wine-making process and a few obligatory samples, we were seated at the family table inside the restaurant on the vineyard grounds. "My grandmother opened this restaurant as a new bride, hoping to bring in more money before the vineyard became so popular. Since then, it has grown in tremendous popularity—especially among the diligent tourists who venture this far," Saggio explained. "If you will allow it, I will select our meal for us."

"Knock yourself out."

"Pardon? 'Knock myself out'?"

"Yeah, sorry, it just an expression we use that means 'go for it' or 'by all means.' It's a good thing!"

"Okay—I will 'knock myself out,'" he said, and we both laughed.

Saggio summoned a waiter, Lorenzo, who was also his cousin, Sofia's son, and began ordering. Soon, slender glasses of bubbling prosecco were presented along with side bowls of green olives, Kalamata olives, and salty Marcona almonds. "I could make a meal off this," I told him as I reached for another few olives.

"There is much still to come," Saggio said. "We have a saying that carries us through our lengthy meals. It says, 'L'appetito vien mangiando' which means, 'the appetite comes while you are eating.'" No sooner had the apertivo been served than additional servers appeared with the antipasti course. Plates heavy with traditional charcuterie meats, cheeses, and bread soon filled our table. "Oh my goodness! This looks delicious," I was almost overcome by the beauty and the bounty of the platters placed in front of us.

"Again, Signore, there will be much more," Saggio warned me with a smile.

"Seriously, this is plenty. I don't need another thing—except maybe a nap!" I was only half-joking.

"Wait, my friend. You will not be disappointed by my family's culinary skills!"

Twenty minutes and another glass of prosecco later, the wait staff replaced the half-empty platters with bowls of steaming risotto, fettucine, and gnocchi. "Ah yes, the primi course—one of my favorites. The risotto comes from the northern regions. This one has bits of lobster mixed throughout. And the fettucine is fresh and house-made served with truffle oil and a delicate parmesan. And the gnocchi is also fresh and comes from my country's northern regions," Saggio explained.

"Saggio, Saggio, Saggio...I'm already about to burst! And you call this lunch? I may not eat until next week!"

"Sit back, rest a bit. Allow your food to settle," Saggio instructed me. "In a few minutes, you will be up for the task before you. I assure you—it is worth the effort! In the meantime, may I excuse myself for a few moments to go and visit with my family members in the kitchen?"

"Knock yourself out," I replied, and we both smiled.

I had to visibly push back from the table to take a break from eating. I looked around to see the restaurant was full of waiting patrons enjoying glasses of wine on the patio. The locals made the rounds to the tables with the handful of tourists asking about their trips, sharing their recommendations, and toasting one another. It was easy to get caught up in the festive and laid-back atmosphere of good food, good drink, and warm and welcoming people. My usual weekday lunch at the deli on the corner was no comparison on so many levels.

In Saggio's absence, our waiter came to refill my half-empty glass of prosecco. "So, that's why I don't know how many glasses I've had," I teased him. "You never let my glass get more than half-empty!"

"It is our practice, signore, to offer exceptional food, drink, and service. We consider your enjoyment our immediate goal," he graciously replied.

Still fascinated by all I had learned from Gianni about Enzo's impact upon his life, I ventured and asked of Lorenzo: "So tell me, Lorenzo, any chance you've met this fellow Enzo I keep hearing about? Sounds like he's some sort of local legend or something."

"Signore, there is no one more generous or kind in all the area than Enzo. He has helped our family insure our heritage and our financial security for generations to come."

"Really? One guy had the power to make sure you and your kids and your kids' kids will be taken care of for the long-haul? How is that possible?"

"Because he invested in our family. He transformed our family restaurant into a worldwide brand. Because of Enzo, the name Pasta Familia is known everywhere as the best pasta sauce in the world."

"Hold up, Lorenzo. Are you telling me the Pasta Familia brand comes out of your kitchen? You gotta be kidding me!"

"Well, technically we don't make the individual batches here anymore, but we did when my grandmother was still alive. Now, we can use our kitchen facilities and restaurant to treat our patrons to the new and delicious dishes we are considering adding to our product line of authentic Italian meals. It is our family's goal to always offer the best dishes we can prepare. That is why people come from all over the world to eat at our table."

"So, where did Enzo come into the picture? What did he do to make all this happen?"

"It wasn't so much what he did to make it happen, because believe me; we have all worked long and hard to accomplish this shared goal; it was more how he set the wheels in motion for this all to happen. He brought influential manufacturers to our restaurant so they could taste for themselves our sauces. He provided guidance when we were ready to begin negotiations with our suppliers and distributors. He also told us early on the value of honoring our heritage in all that we shared with others.

"And he told us never to be consumed with our own successes—to always remember the humble beginnings of our grandmother in her tiny upstairs kitchen who first made the sauce we have become famous for. That is why we all take turns waiting tables and interacting with people such as yourself—it allows us to get honest, real-time feedback from our customers, and it helps to always remind us of the hard work of so many that go into making this operation work so well. For me, I am normally the pastry chef—working with sugar and flour and fillings. But today, I am your server, and it is my privilege. Now, if you'll excuse me, I will bring your next course."

Saggio returned to our table just as Lorenzo stepped away to retrieve the next dishes. He was jubilant from having visited with family members and old friends briefly. "I trust you enjoyed your visit with Lorenzo?" he asked.

"Most definitely," I replied. "I learned more about Enzo and his involvement in this remarkable place. It's like that guy has his hand in everything in these parts."

"He is busy, that is for sure. But it brings him such joy; it is not work for him. He sees it as an investment of all that he has been fortunate to learn and experience. He is famous for saying 'there's no greater investment in life than in the investment in others.'"

Just as Saggio had promised, I was soon able to tackle small servings from each of the bowls on the table. The fresh pasta in the truffle sauce was, without a doubt, one of the best things I have ever tasted in my whole life. Much like the Italian pastries from this morning, I wanted to take some with me, but again thought it might be considered gauche. Instead, I helped myself to a few more small bites.

When we had eaten all we could from the primi course, the waiters took notice and replaced the bowls with smaller platters of beef, chicken, pork, and lamb. "The secondi course!" Saggio announced and signaled for me to help myself.

The meats were a bit easier for me to resist since I couldn't entirely tell how each was prepared. A couple appeared to be roasted, and others sat in puddles of different sauces. I took a small serving of each choice but managed to eat only a few tiny bites.

"Seriously, Saggio, I think I might actually burst!" I told him.

"We will bypass the insalata course to leave room for the formagge e fruita and the dolce courses," Saggio offered in compromise.

"You've got to be kidding me, Saggio, I honestly think I'll be sick if I eat another bite."

"Okay, okay, Signore, I understand. You have reached your limit. I will pay the bill, and we will be on our way."

I offered to pay the bill when it arrived, but Saggio became very animated saying "It will be my honor, you are a guest here."

For almost two hours, I had completely lost track of time, first enjoying the winery tour and then course after course of delicious Italian food. Add to that more refills of prosecco than I bothered to count, and the company of an older gentleman I was fast beginning to consider a friend and mentor, and time had simply gotten away from me…but only temporarily.

While Saggio was paying and saying his extended goodbyes, I thought to check the time on my phone. "Holy smokes! It's after 3:00! Saggio! Come quick—we have got to head towards the factory. *Now, please!*"

shift

Goals give you that sense of meaning and purpose, a clear sense of direction. As you move toward your goals you feel happier and stronger. You feel more energized and effective. You feel more competent and confident in yourself and your abilities.

— Brian Tracy

chapter thirteen

Saggio was quick to answer my urgent summons, and we were in the car and on the road heading toward the Enzo factory five minutes later. We had taken so many winding roads and passed through more than a dozen small towns, I had no clue how far away we were from the factory, but I felt we must be pretty close considering how long we had been driving. I was grateful to be on the road again but was also tremendously frustrated at Saggio for taking the liberty of consuming so much of my day and possibly endangering my tour.

In the meantime, though, I had grown quite fond of my new friend and his relatable philosophies on life, some of which had already given me some serious pause for thought. Saggio seemed to have lived a good life to this point, though, if I were truly honest with myself. I couldn't help but wonder why such a seemingly wise and intelligent man had settled for driving other people around. Where was the recognition and pay-off in taking other people to *their* important meetings?

I could hardly help myself, continually checking the time on my phone…3:20 p.m.….3:30 p.m…and then, Saggio slowed to make the sharp left turn onto a small side road that was bordered on both sides by plentiful orchards. On the left were row after row of lemon trees and on the right bountiful Clementine trees spread out as far as I could see. I was so taken by the endless rows of fruit trees, all heavy with ripening fruit, that I didn't even see the factory until we were nearly upon it. A friendly elderly gentleman greeted us at the check-in station. He reached into shake Saggio's hand before waving us through and raising the barricade arm.   Saggio slowed to a roll and pulled into what appeared to be a designated parking area. By the time he had parked, more than a dozen factory workers had gathered to welcome him.

I figured either Saggio made this drive on a regular basis or these guys were all his cousins or something.
"Buongiorno, friends," Saggio greeted his friends, hugging and air-kissing each one. "Today, I have important business, but I will be back tomorrow, and we will all visit more then—*va bene*?" The group nodded collectively as they dispersed and headed to their respective cars to leave.

"Where are they all going?" "It is approaching 4-o'clock, quitting time," Saggio replied. "They come to work early to allow them more time in the evening with their families. It is very, very important to our culture to spend as much time as we are able with the ones we love the most."

"Yeah, but 4:00? I wouldn't have lasted a week in my job if I'd have even thought about clocking out at four."

"It is a difference in values, my friend. We do what we must to be able to do what we want, and for my people, that means choosing long meals and lots of laughter over having too many possessions. That is how we consider a man rich—by his time spent with others."

And then I quickly realized that my tour might be in danger. "If they're all leaving, is there anyone left to give me a tour?"

"Most assuredly. Those were a few of the craftsmen and women who work in the factory. The people you came to meet with are still here."

Saggio led me across the parking lot to a two-story stone building that more resembled a large, stately manor than a professional workspace. Individual windows on both floors spanned from end to end, each with black shutters on either side. We walked towards two large, black wooden doors and a sign that read, "Tutti sono benvenuti" with translations in English, French, and German below it. "Everyone is welcome," it read.

Once inside, the receptionist greeted Saggio warmly and extended her hand to me, "I am Anna. I will tell the team of your arrival."

Immediately, I could hear the click-clack of heels striking the marble floor and conversations becoming clearer as six men and women seemed to take their place in a line in front of Saggio and myself.

"Today, I have the privilege of bringing Signore David Jericho, from Bowman + Leonard in the United States, for a tour of the Enzo factory. I will leave him in your competent hands to show him around," Saggio said as he handed me off to the official Enzo people.

The men and women all nodded, and one by one stepped forward to introduce themselves, "I am Alessandro, Mr. Jericho, welcome to Enzo."

"I am Stefano, pleased to meet you."

"I am Sofia. We are glad you are here."

The progression continued until I had met each one. "Thank you all for such a warm welcome," I offered, very impressed with their professionalism. "Now, please don't ask me to recite every name back to you all!" My shortcoming with names seemed to lighten the mood as they all laughed at my confession.

"Perhaps tomorrow, we will have badges to help you remember better," one woman offered kindly.

"That's not a half-bad idea!" I welcomed the idea.

A 50-ish woman stepped forward and reintroduced herself for my benefit. "Again, I am Valentina, the Factory Director, and I will have the pleasure of showing you around our facility today." The rest of the team members had only come to make their initial introductions and to welcome me. I thanked them for the introductions and told them I looked forward to visiting with them further the next morning as they stepped away.

I thought it unusual as they all collectively went to visit Saggio, but again, figured it was just out of familiarity and friendliness. The laughter and camaraderie they shared with one another, *even the company driver*, was a far cry from the usual atmosphere at B +L.

"Shall we?" Valentina asked as she motioned me forward.

In a flash of panic, I suddenly realized that, beyond the tour, I had failed to check my itinerary for the specifics about the rest of the day and night. As Valentina and I began to walk toward the factory door, we passed the reception area and were interrupted by Anna, "Scuzzi, Valentina, Signore Jericho—Saggio wanted me to inform you both that there is no need to hurry and that I am to call him when you are ready to be picked up and delivered to the hotel."

It was as if Saggio had read my mind. I was greatly relieved to know my ride and accommodations were in order and able to give my full attention to Valentina as she led the way towards the Enzo factory.

As soon as Valentina opened the thick steel door to a secured area of the factory, I was overcome by the strong smell of leather. "This smells like a men's cologne...on steroids!" I thought to myself. My face must have given me away as Valentina turned towards me, "It is something you get used to—the smell, that is. Like you, I was almost overcome by it in the beginning; now I don't even notice it," she said graciously.

"I'll keep that in mind," I said as I wiped my watering eyes and smiled.

"At Enzo, maintaining our company culture is of utmost importance to us," Valentina began. "We have had many offers in the past—especially from American companies—to increase our sales 10, 15, even 20 times more, but always at the expense of what we value most—our heritage, our deep commitment to preserving the integrity of our craftsmanship, and the welfare of our employees who are as family to us.

"Most of the companies who come to visit us and who seek to do business with us come with plans to tell us what they can do for us, *not inquiring as to what we want* of the partnership. And so, the answer has always been 'No.'"

I could feel a pit in the bottom of my stomach. Everything about how my company did business was precisely *not* what Enzo was looking for—from the proposal to the terms of service to the non-negotiables, B + L was just another in a long line of suitors courting a company with completely opposing cultures.

My mind was racing as I raffled through the options I had regarding tomorrow's presentation—present the standard B + L, by-the-book proposal and by some stroke of good fortune, win the account; or go rogue and present my personal pitch and risk the consequences.

"These are the dying vats where we mix custom colors for each of our European distributors. We hope to do the same when we decide to expand to North America." Valentina was already ten steps ahead of me, pointing to huge vats of different colored dyes.

"When we go upstairs, you will be able to look down into them and see the different colors. We are always experimenting with different combinations here, looking to create the most robust color possible for our products. It is one of the many aspects of our company that sets us apart from so many of the other leather goods houses."

Valentina's pride in her company was apparent from the start. Her involvement in Enzo seemed to be personal. She went well beyond just quoting the company lingo; she took tremendous pride in it and seemed to feel a sense of responsibility to represent it as best as possible. On the other hand, I began to feel like a fraud, unsure of what I believed about much of anything anymore—including how I felt about how my company did business. The comparison between Enzo and B + L was as stark as the difference between Valentina and me. She was proud of her company, and I was little more than a middle-aged, middle management schmuck who had been reduced to doing nothing more than reciting the company brochure for years. Way too many years.

An hour-and-a-half later, we returned to our original starting point, the secured steel door that led us back outside. "And that is our processes in a nutshell," Valentina said, signaling the end of the tour. "Certainly, there are many intricacies beyond what I showed you today, but hopefully, you have a better idea about how and why our quality leather goods are so much more than simply seasonal handbags or wallets or shoes. They are an investment. Much of what we do could be automated, and to some extent, we have allowed moderate mechanization of some of the lesser important steps, but our personal involvement with everything bearing the Enzo name is what we value most. That, and the tremendous value we place on our employees and the villages and towns they come from. Their well-being is our well-being.

shift

"Our pay scale is very generous, but our actions as a company go well beyond that. We believe our next generation of designers, craftsmen and women, and company leadership, is in the villages that surround us. That is why we do much to benefit their lives."

"May I ask how you came to join the Enzo company and have you been here long?"

"Oh yes," she replied happily. "Mine is a story almost too good to believe."

She had my complete attention now. "By all means, I would love to hear it."

"As I explained, much of our workforce, across all lines of responsibility within the company, comes from nearby towns and villages. It has always been tremendously crucial for Enzo to turn first to our neighbors whenever we are making new hires. That is how I first came to the company.

"While still in secondary school, I began working in the factory several days a week when school was over for the day. My parents urged me to work and gain experience and possibly even a skill before considering university. They wanted me to have an idea of what interested me before I enrolled.

"I enjoyed my time at the factory, watching the products come together, and knowing they would be enjoyed by women the world over, but I wanted to do something more than just assembling our products. I began sketching new designs in my spare time, sometimes just adding minor details to our current styles, sometimes creating completely different designs. I would lose track of time when I began sketching— often having to be called to dinner repeatedly by my madre," she grimaced as she explained.

"Eventually, I became bold enough to share a few of my drawings with our lead designer who liked them so much she shared them with Enzo. As a schoolgirl still, I was nervous even at the suggestion I could design, but Enzo saw the potential in my work and placed several of my sketches in the production line for the upcoming season.

"When they were very well-received by our customers, I was offered a full-time position on the design team upon graduation. It was like a dream. Since then, I have been promoted first to lead designer upon the retirement of our previous lead and eventually, to where I am now to oversee all areas of the factory operations. My experience in the factory helped lay the groundwork for me to understand the many intricacies of our products, the many, many steps involved in the production process, and come to appreciate our company's unwavering dedication to producing the highest quality purses and leather goods possible. There are many shortcuts we could take, but the cost to our integrity is much too high.

"And that is how I have come to my present role—all because Enzo believed in my simple designs enough to make them available to the world."

I was almost speechless listening to Valentina describe her career path and the culture of her company and the intention with which they operated their company. Clearly, many things were more important than money to them. And the promise of being in every mainstream suburban mall in America was, without a doubt, at odds with their culture's priorities.

Back inside the office, we were joined by Luca, Gianna, Alessandro, and Sofia. They each reintroduced themselves and shared which area of the company they were involved in. After a few more rounds of small talk—the nearby sites, the villages, the wineries—they each extended their hand to thank me for my time and interest in their company and to tell me they were looking forward to discussing my proposal in person the following morning.

As they each turned to leave, Anna from the receptionist's desk signaled for me to come across to her workstation. "I am preparing to leave for the day, but I have notified Saggio that your tour is complete. He is expected to be here within five minutes."

"Grazzi," I nodded in appreciation and turned to make my exit just where I had entered a couple of hours earlier. Just as I reached for the large brass doorknob, I heard the dulcet tones of the vintage Ferrari V8 coming down the main road. The sound was almost magical, echoing off the main building and the factory walls.

"I trust my friends here were helpful to you, Signore Jericho?" Saggio asked as he pulled up and I got in.

"Yes, yes—not a question left unanswered. It is an amazing group of people. And Valentina could not have done a better job of walking me through the entire production process."

"It is always good to hear the Enzo people are always exceeding the expectations of those they meet with. Tell me, Signore Jericho, would you like to join me and some of the Enzo team you just met for dinner, possibly around 8:00 p.m.? I have known the families of so many of the people you met today for many, many years and we have made arrangements to visit again this evening. However, if you feel you must rest or further prepare, do not hesitate to do so as we will all understand."

"Are you kidding?" I said. A chance to schmooze the client a little bit longer? "Count me in!" I surprised even myself with my enthusiastic reply. "I might even rest my eyes for a while and review all I've learned today. And it will be another few hours before I can even consider eating again after the lunch we had. In fact, I think I recall saying I wasn't going to eat for another week!" I almost felt powerless over the temptation of another indulgent meal.

"Va Bene! I will let them know you will be joining us. But for now, I will take you to your hotel for the night and introduce you to the Fabbri family. They own and operate an exceptional family inn, the Hotel Piccinelli, and will take excellent care of you. It is only a short drive from here."

"You know, Saggio, I'm curious about something. When I look at the map on my phone, it appears we went really far out of the way when we left Gianni's auto shop to get here. Why did we take the small, out-of-the-way road to get there?" I had to know his reason.

shift

"Well, Signore Jericho, you are correct—the highway was an option. One option. But I wanted you to be able to take in the countryside, admire the vineyards, and appreciate the beauty that is my country."

"But that added more than an hour to our route. Weren't you concerned about getting me to my appointment in time?"

"I knew precisely where we were traveling and how long the journey would take. You must remember, these roads are my home. I am well acquainted with the highway system, but I much prefer the ways that fill my soul—*that* you cannot receive when you are traveling 200 kilometers per hour…even though that's fun too.

"You know as well as I do that there are usually many options for reaching a destination. The highways are often the obvious routes, intended to suit many people at one time. But because so many make this choice, it also brings with it many problems—collisions, road construction, congestion, detours. In this case, the obvious choice has many hazards associated with it.

"There are also smaller, less conspicuous, and less traveled roads that will take you where you need to go. However, to find these, you must seek them out to discover where they lead and decide if they are a better option for you. The reward for your effort can come in ways you could never expect. The obvious path may be the easiest to pursue, at least in the beginning, but it frequently brings with it concessions and consequences. Many roads may get you to your destination, but often, the less traveled road is the most satisfying. You will never regret investigating the options available to you when they are available."

"You seem to have some practical advice for every dilemma I'm facing," I marveled. "I wish I had met you about ten years ago—before I started down this dead-end road called my career. Maybe I wouldn't be in this situation if I'd met you earlier."

"You are at a turning point, Signore. From what you have told me of your problems, you still have many options to choose from. You are not in as hopeless a situation as you believe," Saggio wasn't letting me off the hook too easily.

A few minutes later, we pulled in to the Hotel Piccinelli and were greeted by the proprietor himself, Signore Fabbri. He and Saggio embraced before Saggio turned to introduce me to what appeared to be another long-time friend. "Come, come," Signore Fabbri said as he waved us inside to check in. The hotel was a far cry from the luxurious resort in Milan, but it was much better suited for my tastes. In all my years of traveling, I had never come to view my expense report as a means to overindulge on the company's dime. If I hadn't personally paid for where I was staying, I wouldn't stay there when I was out on business either. It was my litmus test as to whether a hotel was out of my league.

After a quick check-in, Signore Fabbri led the way up a narrow staircase to the third floor where he showed me to my room. He confirmed dinner reservations at Campollo's was at 8:00 p.m. adding, "It is the best restaurant in all of Italy. They are known throughout the entire Emilia-Romagna region for their fresh Parmesan cheese, ricotta, and pizza…va bene."

"Ahhh! Now there's a word I recognize—pizza!" I exclaimed, and we all laughed.

shift

"I will leave you to your room. Please, don't hesitate to call the front desk if anything is lacking. Otherwise, I will hope to see you later this evening, perhaps," Signore Fabbri said as he took his leave.

"So, I should meet you in the lobby just before 8:00 p.m.?" I asked as Saggio opened his door.

"Yes. Until then," he said as he nodded goodbye.

I knew I should probably check my proposals and make sure the other presentation details were in order, but I also wanted to be refreshed for this unexpected opportunity for more face time with the Enzo people. I was uncharacteristically tired for it not even being 6:00 p.m., but attributed it to the carryover effects from the jet lag as well as the stress I'd been through most of the day, just worrying about making it to my appointment in time.

Sleep won out over additional preparation as I set my phone alarm for an hour-and-a-half. "After all," I reasoned, "I can always get back to it after dinner."

The nap did me good, and even Saggio looked a bit refreshed himself when we met in the lobby at 7:55. "I trust you rested well," asked Saggio.

"I definitely did. I think I was still short on sleep after my flight and the change in time zones. But now…now I feel much better."

"And I pray your appetite has returned since our generous lunch?"

"Yes, but, do you think we could keep it a little simpler tonight—maybe a salad and pizza? I don't know how you all eat so, so much and don't end up weighing 400 pounds!"

"Some of us do," added Saggio. "Wait until you see Adolpho, the chef. He must taste everything before it leaves the kitchen!" I had to laugh at the image of a roly-poly Italian chef.

We arrived at the restaurant just as Valentina, Alessandro, and Gianna were being seated. "Buonasera," Saggio said as he and I approached the table.

"Buonasera," they echoed.

"I must warn you all," Saggio began, "that Signore Jericho has requested we have a somewhat simpler meal this evening. Apparently, he was a bit overwhelmed by our many courses and generous servings at lunch." Everyone laughed when I nodded in agreement.

"It's true," I said, "you're looking at a guy who is used to a burger and fries for a meal, or maybe just a salad if my wife is trying to get me to eat healthier," and again they laughed.

"We would like to consider you our guests tonight, if you would allow," Valentina proposed.

"I thought I was the one trying to win your business. Isn't that the usual order of how things are done—that I should cover dinner?"

"Perhaps traditionally, but we prefer to cover our expenses and those of our guests. It helps us maintain our integrity in decision-making and prevents us from being beholden to anyone."

shift

"Admirable," I commended her. "Most companies in America see it just the opposite—they believe, 'if you want my business, treat me to a fancy meal, send me nice gifts, take me on a trip.' I admire your commitment to strong values. And you're right—it keeps from muddying up the waters."

"Thank you for allowing us to honor our practices. And now, I think we all need wine!" Valentina signaled the waiter and ordered several carafes for the table. At the same time, she ordered several antipasto plates for the table as appetizers.

Five minutes later, our glasses were full, and everyone had relaxed considerably. We took turns jockeying for our favorite items on the antipasto plates. "These cheeses are the best I've ever tasted," I began. "What am I saying? *Everything* is the best I've ever tasted!" My dinner companions nodded in hearty agreement.

As Saggio recommended the *Caprino Fresco* cheese, he leaned over and whispered, "I know how to make that."

I remembered how he had shared that he had learned to milk goats as a boy. I couldn't help but smile at his suggestion and said, "Well, in that case, pass some over, I need to try it."

It was amazingly fresh and like nothing I had ever tasted before. "Wow! Saggio, this is amazing." He nodded knowingly, as if to say, "I told you so."

With a somewhat captive audience, I turned my attention to learning more about them, their company, and their values. "Tell me, what do you all attribute the tremendous success of the Enzo brand and all its products to? You mentioned your attention to remaining impartial and protecting your personal integrity, but what is it about the company that makes it so exceptional?"

Valentina, Alessandro, and Gianna all looked at one another as if to ask who would answer first. Alessandro took the lead and began, "Signore Jericho, the integrity is the bedrock of our company—our personal integrity as well as the company's because *we are the company.* If we are unable to maintain our integrity for ourselves, we have no hope of carrying it into our business dealings.

"Each of us has many responsibilities—at work and home, but we have all learned from Enzo the importance of focus— focus on the matter at hand and focus on the purpose behind it. When you understand the real purpose of what you are charged with doing, it makes it considerably easier to address it, solve it, remove it, or delegate it. Otherwise, we find ourselves starting many projects—too many projects, giving none of them our undivided attention, and seeing nothing excellently done to completion."

"I hear you on that," I couldn't help but commiserate. "It seems like I spend most of my days putting out fires—handling one crisis after another. At the end of the day, I wonder where the time went and what I really accomplished."

"We have felt that tug too," Gianna jumped in. "But we have come to see the wisdom of focusing on the purpose of our positions. Why place such an emphasis on the well-being of our employees? Why pay such attention to the smallest detail? Why involve all levels of employees in the design process?

We believe we were all created for a purpose and when you find yours, you will be satisfied and productive. That is why we work so closely with everyone on our team. When we can answer these questions, progress is greater and smoother. Some days, it is an easy practice; other days, it is much more difficult, but we have all come to appreciate the value of the practice. Everyone who is a part of the Enzo family understands the purpose of what we are all a part of—and that is to produce the finest, most beautiful leather goods the world has ever known. When we remember the purpose of it all, everything we do becomes more compelling."

I was taking in every word. This habit of understanding the purpose behind everything was quite intriguing. It seemed so obvious, and yet I had never heard it explained in this manner. It was also evident this was a deeply ingrained company practice. But it seemed even more than that; it was almost a lifestyle. These were not merely company employees quoting the corporate tagline; this was something each of them clearly believed was the key to the company's success. "It's either all true, or this is some kind of mind trick they've all been led to believe," I told myself.

"It's quite impressive—your shared beliefs in what makes your company so unique. It is rare to find such wholehearted buy-in in any company or organization these days. So many people today are more focused on wanting to be known for *their* ideas, *their* actions, *their* innovations that it makes it difficult to achieve true organizational cohesiveness. That whole 'focus on the purpose' concept could really get in the way of individual egos, I imagine."

Alessandro was quick to clarify: "To be clear, we do not discourage individuality, individual excellence, or individual identity—actually quite the opposite—we embrace and encourage it. It is the understanding and support of our collective purpose that matters most to our company. When our employees understand its importance, they are free to develop and create and fulfill at will. It is very empowering when that is your only constraint."

Throughout the night, our waiters' attention was relentless—they had replaced our near-empty carafes with full ones and traded out our sparse charcuterie trays with three huge pizzas cooked in wood-fired brick ovens that looked like they were hundreds of years old. The service was so seamless and the conversation so engaging across the table; we all ate and drank and talked almost non-stop for three hours. It wasn't until I could begin to feel the warming sensation of the wine taking effect that I realized I was nearing my limit of alcohol.

"Well, ladies and gentlemen, at this rate, it will be less than 12 hours before we meet again—though, presumably, next time will be without all this incredible food and wine! In the interest of representing my company as best as I possibly can tomorrow morning, I think I should probably turn in for the evening," I told my hosts as I pushed my plate aside.

My dinner companions nodded in agreement and stood to leave also. Valentina, Alessandro, and Gianna gave both Saggio and me warm hugs goodnight and walked to their cars. Saggio and I walked the half block back to our hotel, offering each other a good night's rest before retiring to our respective rooms.

shift

I couldn't be sure if my relaxed state of mind were from the wine or the satisfaction from having learned a good deal more about the Enzo culture, but either way, I was beginning to feel at ease with these people, what they valued, and how they ran their business. It was a vast improvement over frantic, chase-the-next-big-thing way things were handled at B + L.

Before I turned in for the night, I stopped to process all that had happened that day and could hardly believe my adventures with Saggio had only just begun earlier in the day. "Man, that guy packs a lot of living into one day," I thought. "He saw more old friends and family today than I do in a year! The kids in Gianni's village love him, the workers at the factory consider him a friend, and everywhere we went—*for miles and miles!*

All I could figure was that Saggio's life as a driver must have taken him many, many places throughout the years and as a result, he had gotten to know many people from many different places. He even reminded me somewhat of a well-connected concierge at a large resort—he knew everybody and everybody knew him.

But I couldn't settle one thing—just because Saggio was well-traveled didn't necessarily explain why he was so incredibly well-received *by so many.* I knew lots of people back home who were well known but not particularly well-loved or even well-liked.I reeled through the comments and insights Saggio had shared with me unbelievably just since 9:00 a.m. *this morning.* He wasn't quoting the trendiest leadership book on the market; he was speaking *what he knew* and *what he had lived.* What I had initially considered folksy, even homespun, philosophies and perspectives, I was now coming to realize was actually relevant and applicable principles.

And not just for an old Italian driver.

But for a desperate, fearful, middle-aged guy from Texas.

shift

*True stability results when
presumed order and presumed
disorder are balanced.
A truly stable system expects
the unexpected,
is prepared to be disrupted,
waits to be transformed.*

– Tom Robbins

chapter fourteen

I was up early the next morning shaving, showering, and packing up to leave for the airport following my presentation. I had a schedule to keep and knew I'd be at my best if I had something in my stomach before visiting with the Enzo team. I took a table for two in the hotel's small dining area.

In broken English, the waiter asked what I would have to drink and directed me to the breakfast buffet area. Fortunately, though, that still meant a grand selection of fresh baked breakfast rolls and pastries that was promptly delivered to my table with a small crock of farm-fresh butter and locally crafted jams and jellies.

Once done, I signed the bill and went to turn in my room key and check-out at the front desk. "Buongiorno Signore Jericho," Mr. Fabbri greeted me.

shift

"Buongiorno, Signore Fabbri," I tried my hand at repeating his accent.

"May I ask how your stay with us was? And your breakfast this morning?"

"Couldn't have been better!" I told him enthusiastically. "And the breakfast—how do you say 'delicious'?"

"Ah, delizioso!" Fabbri replied.

"Yes, yes, delizioso! By the way, have you seen Saggio this morning? I am needing to get to the Enzo headquarters soon and thought I'd see him down here by now."

"Si, Signore Jericho. He asked that I inform you that he has arranged for an Uber driver to get you to the Enzo Company. He is here now and waiting for you just outside the entrance."

"B-b-b-ut what happened to Saggio? I certainly would have said 'goodbye' to him and thanked him for everything if I knew I wasn't going to see him again." I was almost speechless at the abrupt change in plans. And honestly, I was a little disappointed that he left without saying 'goodbye' at least.

"Oh no, Signore Jericho—you will probably see him again, he said. He is always coming and going from the factory."

"O-o-okay," I said as I rebounded from the thought of not getting to fully thank Saggio for all he had done and taught me. "I certainly hope so."

"Yes, yes—he will be there. He gave his word."

"Well, in that case, I had better meet my new driver. Thank you for everything—it was a delightful stay."

Just as Mr. Fabbri had said, a tall, young Italian man was standing outside the large wooden doors of the entrance. "Signore Jericho?" he asked when he saw me.

"Yes—that's me. And you're my driver?"

"Si, signore. I am Matteo, and I will take you to the Enzo factory whenever you are ready."

"In that case, Matteo, let's go," I said, now able to relax a bit after the reassurance of seeing Saggio again.

I climbed into Matteo's micro sedan, a far cry from Saggio's Ferrari, and didn't have it in me to engage in conversation with Matteo the way I had with Saggio. Instead, I reflected on my most memorable day with Saggio and wanted to thank him more than ever. I was just begging to grasp the impact he had had on me in such a short time.

The trip to the factory took about 10 minutes, and as I entered the building, I was greeted by Anna before the doors closed behind me.

"It is good to see you again so soon, Signore Jericho."

"Anna, right?"

"Very good! I see you have an excellent memory," she responded, flattered that I remembered from the day before. "Would you like to leave your suitcase with me for safekeeping while you are meeting?"

"That would wonderful—one less thing to worry about."

"Allow me," she said taking it from me and placing it behind the large wooden desk that was her space. "And now, I will show you to our conference room. Our team is ready for you."

I followed her closely and could see a mostly full conference room through the glass just beyond a suite of offices. "Looks like the gang's all here!" I said, trying not to sound too anxious as the weight of the presentation I was about to make came bearing down on me. Up until this point, I had felt confident in knowing the talking points of the proposal so well. And I couldn't help but think I'd undoubtedly scored some serious points after last night's dinner with some of the Enzo employees. Still, after all my years of doing this, I came to expect the moments right before a pitch to always be a bit tense, kind of like what a veteran performer still feels just before he takes the stage.

I surveyed the room as we approached the door, grateful to see all the familiar faces from yesterday, plus a few additional ones. Valentina was waiting at the door and was the first to greet me. She ushered me in and announced my arrival to the room: "Signore Jericho, so very good to see you again. Ladies and gentlemen, I have the privilege of presenting our friend, Mr. David Jericho, from Bowman + Leonard in the United States. He is the one responsible for the proposal we received earlier in the week. We are looking forward to hearing further about the ideas in your proposal." Everyone had since taken their seat around the table nodded and appreciatively, most of them even smiling.

"Thank you, thank you," I opened up while trying to get a read on the room. Everyone around the table seemed entirely focused on what I was about to say, something that wasn't always the case in these kinds of situations. I took it as a good sign, hoping they were at least starting off on my side—a huge benefit I had come to appreciate after making hundreds of these presentations through the years.

"Don't blow this, Jericho," I told myself as I took a deep breath.

As I scanned the room, I noticed a vacant seat at the far end of the table, the spot usually reserved for the most senior member of the team. Was it a power play to leave it open? Would Valentina take her seat there? Was there someone still to come? My mind was reeling with possibilities.

"I am eager to share my company's ideas with you all and hope to begin a mutually beneficial relationship with your company in the very near future. I think our partnership with Enzo…" Valentina stepped forward to interrupt: "I am sorry for the confusion, Signore Jericho," she began to apologize. "We will begin in just a moment because we have the pleasure of having the head of our company, Signore Enzo Pastorelli, join us today. It is rare for Signore Pastorelli to review a presentation with our team as he usually trusts us to act in the best interest of the company; however, today, he expressed a deep interest in hearing your presentation."

"Wow! That's wonderful. I don't know what to say," I was both flattered and floundering for the right words, wanting to be appreciative without gushing too much. Even though I had learned much about Signore Pastorelli, I still didn't feel I had gotten a complete picture of what he was really about—at least regarding how it related to bringing his company's products to the US. Suddenly, I felt totally unprepared. Barry had told me he was *the* key to the deal, and his decision would be the deal-maker…or *deal breaker*. I was grateful he would be in attendance but took his being late as not a good sign for me.

shift

"How about I take this opportunity to distribute additional copies of my proposal. This one is 'hot off the press' as they say—concerning our potential partnership between B + L and your team here at Enzo."

I reached inside my computer bag and grabbed the stack of official proposals, what Barry had considered being the showpiece of the B + L presentation package. Walking the room and personally handing off a copy to each person gave me an opportunity to burn off a little nervous energy as well as make eye contact with each person individually.

Just as I handed the final copy out, I looked up to see Saggio standing in the doorway smiling broadly. "Sag-g-g-i-o, what are you doing…" Questions were filling my mind faster than I could process them. *"What is happening? Who is this man?"*

Saggio came in and embraced Valentina with a traditional Italian triple cheek kiss and then took his seat in the head chair at the far end of the conference table—*the one reserved for the highest in authority.* Stefano turned and said, "Senior Pastorelli, vuoi dell'acqua naturale?"

All I heard was Pastorelli…the Enzo Pastorelli, founder of Enzo. The guy I spent the day with was the CEO? And I didn't have a clue? "This is not happening to me," was all I could think. "This absolutely cannot be happening. Suddenly, I recalled everything I revealed to Saggio about my job, my company, my *life!* "I am screwed, I am beyond screwed. I am so far beyond it; I don't even know which way is up." I struggled to regain my composure, but it wasn't easy. "But, I thought you were Saggio, my driver. You run a company, *and* you drive people around?"

I knew it didn't make sense even as I said it, but it was the only sentence I could piece together. And even though I didn't intend for it to be funny, several chuckled at my assumption.

"Well, only for very special people, do I drive them around personally," Enzo conceded. "But it was because several of the points in the proposal you sent us intrigued me, and I wanted to get to know more about you before we arrived at this point."

"So, you're *not* Saggio, you're really Enzo?" and again those in the conference room smiled at my gradual realization.

"I am Enzo—through and through. And these are the leaders of our company who have helped to make it possible for our fine company to continuing standing for what we have always stood for—honor, integrity, and the highest quality leather goods available," he said as he nodded approvingly to those seated around the table.

Enzo took his seats and nodded for me to begin. "Where were we…before I got the surprise of my life?" I asked out loud as my onlookers smiled and reengaged. "Get back on that horse, Jericho," I kept repeating in my mind. "Get back on the horse and do what you came here to do and then get the hell outta Dodge."

I did my best to pull myself together and began with my usual overview of B + L. I listed our highest profile clients, talked up our range of services, the strength of our corporate leadership, and the integrated support our regional offices provided. From there, I went straight to the crux of the proposal, explaining our established history and how B + L was superior from our competitors as well as our optimistic projection of what we could do for Enzo.

shift

I noticed halfway through my spiel the mood of the room seemed to take an unmistakable downward turn. I couldn't put my finger on what caused it, but it was evident the pleasant smiles, and agreeable nods had been replaced with blank and stoic stares from some; furrowed and concerned brows from the others. Something was up; I just didn't know what it was...yet.

It wasn't until I referenced a graph on page 5 of the proposal that it became evident there had been a mistake—a grave mistake—in the transmission of the intended proposal I had sent on Monday from the airport.

"Which proposal?" Sofia asked.

"I do not see a graph in my copy," Stefano added.

"Try the other one, Stefano," suggested Alessandro. "Which one are you speaking from, Signore Jericho?"

I was dumbfounded. Speechless. And I thought I was going to be sick. Had I really sent the wrong version--*my version* of the proposal by mistake? The one with all my grandiose ideas about customized client programs? And extensive involvement every step of the way to the retail customers? The very ideas Barry had shut down immediately, going so far as to accuse me of 'giving away the company' because of my ridiculous ideas about concentrating on client service above maintaining the profit margin?

"I cannot believe this is happening," I mumbled to myself. All I could think was that my whole career, hell, *my whole life*, was literally imploding right in front of me. What was I going to tell Jenny? And the girls? And Barry? A million thoughts were racing through my mind—and *all of them were catastrophic.*

There would be absolutely no recovering from a mistake of this size. It was unbelievable…freakin' unbelievable. In a flash of a second, I even wondered if it was really an honest mistake or was it something more. Maybe a Freudian slip of my overactive ego? No, it absolutely couldn't have been. No matter how weak I considered the official B + L proposal, I could honestly say I would never have knowingly gone rogue and substituted my idealistic version instead of the official company pitch—especially under these circumstances. That much I was sure of.

A few seconds later, I gathered my wits and dove into action—the only action I thought could save my job. I walked the perimeter of the conference table asking to collect the erroneously sent version—*my version*—and apologized profusely to each person who surrendered one to me. "But, this was so different from what we are used to seeing," Alessandro contested.

"You presented ideas and services no one has ever offered to us before. We were intrigued—all of us," added Sofia. The entire table nodded in agreement.

"Can't you honor this first proposal we received? Or at least present it and explain some of the options you mentioned involving what you called…I believe you referred to it as 'a genuine partnership'—right here on the introduction page.'" Valentina was giving me one more out, one more opportunity to reconsider which proposal I stood by—the standard-issue company playbook or the unique and customized version I had sent by mistake.

shift

"You know, under different circumstances, perhaps I would feel the freedom to veer from our some of the offerings of our traditional presentation, but at this moment, I don't feel like I should take that liberty. Perhaps, if you all are seriously inclined to partner with B + L, some of the minor aspects of the proposal could be altered—maybe deleted, edited, or possibly even enhanced. But short of being able to convey to my company your intent to move forward with an agreement, it is doubtful I could or should make any significant adjustments." I was doing my best impersonation of a sold-out company man but was convincing no one in the conference room, including myself.

"Even if it means closing the door on a possible working relationship with Enzo?" Valentina lobbed one more soft pitch across the plate—an easy hit with an obvious answer. It killed me to have to let it fly past, but truly felt I had no choice in the matter. Company loyalty was the last piece of personal dignity I could cling to at this point. "I'm afraid not. The management team above me is concerned that offering such extensive accommodations for your company will lead to others demanding it too. Before long, every client will be coming at us with their own private set of demands, each wanting something more than the company before them—just a case of human nature—to want what your neighbor has...*plus a little bit more.*

"Our traditional proposals have been industry standards for decades. To change their language, their tone, or even the whole intent is not something on our current management's radar. They have other, more urgent and more pressing, concerns before them at the moment—changing something that has worked for years and years just isn't top of their list right now."

"That's unfortunate, Signore Jericho, because we found your initial proposal so promising and so hopeful for how we seek to do business with others," said Valentina, accepting defeat.

"Please accept my most heartfelt apology for this gross misunderstanding," I began. "This first, erroneously-sent proposal is independent of my association with Bowman + Leonard. It is nothing more than the idle thoughts of a man with little sleep and under tremendous personal pressure. If I could undo my mistake, I would do so immediately, but as it is, I consider it my responsibility to present what I was charged to present; anything significantly different would be beyond my scope as a representative of Bowman + Leonard. But, I wholeheartedly ask for your indulgence as I present the intended presentation."

I was making a final plea as well.

Before she could respond, Enzo stood and addressed the room: "My friends, Signore Jericho has told us of his limitations despite our requests otherwise. As such, I would like to thank you all for your time and ask that you allow us to visit privately."

The Enzo team members took their collective cue and filed out of the room quickly, leaving their remaining proposals on the conference room table. Valentina was the last to leave, turning to me before exiting: "Signore Jericho, it was a pleasure showing you our facility yesterday and dinner later on. I wish you safe travels back home and continued success with your company," and then she was gone.

shift

Enzo and I stood facing one another from opposite ends of the conference table. "Please...sit," Enzo suggested, and I readily accepted, nearly collapsing into the closest chair. "David, I must tell you how surprised and disappointed I am in how this meeting turned out. It was because of your original proposal that I wanted to get to know you better in the first place. Without the titles and roles of each other getting in the way, I hoped we could form an authentic business friendship at the least, and possibly a profitable and mutually beneficial business partnership at best."

I was beginning to feel like a kid called into the principal's office for skipping school—angry at getting caught, embarrassed to have disappointed, and remorseful for carrying out an ill-conceived plan. I tried to maintain eye-to-eye contact with Enzo but ultimately found it much easier to look down.

"David, you captured my interest in your initial proposal—what I understand to be *your* proposal...Correct?" I nodded in agreement. "The ideas presented in this first presentation were innovative and exactly in line with where I am taking this company. They offered considerations that expressly conveyed your company's interest in *enhancing* our business, not a list of mandatory processes for us to do business with your company. Your opening remarks showed our team that you had a clear understanding of and appreciation for our products, our company, and the values we stand for. Your philosophy of serving generously, beyond the scope of the contract, if needed, particularly piqued our interest as that is a core value of my company.

"That proposal...that is the proposal we would have accepted."

"But that's not what I am being paid to represent," I countered. "Saggio, er...Enzo, this secondary proposal that I brought with me today—that is the proposal I am charged with representing, not my independent ideas outside of the office."

"I appreciate your loyalty, David, but I can't help but wonder what your boss would tell you to do as things stand. Nothing? Maintain your commitment to the unimaginative standard proposal for ease and continuity? Or venture beyond the corporate boundaries in order to win a world-class account? Tell me, David, what do you think he would say?"

"I-I-I don't know," I said quietly. "I honestly don't know. Every attempt I have made at trying to reframe our proposals by focusing more personalized service has been met with complete rejection. And not just a thanks-for-the-suggestion kind of rejection, but an all-out case-closed, don't-ever-mention-this-nonsense-again kind of rejection."

"That tells me everything I need to know about your company and their business practices," Enzo explained. "Now, I have a much better understanding of what your company values and their willingness—or rather lack of desire—to accommodate those with whom they do business.

"As for you, David, my advice is simple: in order to make the changes in your life you told me about yesterday, you must be willing to take ownership for what you know to be right—above and beyond so-called company guidelines. It will not always be

shift

the easy path to take, but it will always be the *right* one. And, more importantly, you will be much better equipped to face the man staring back at you from the mirror each morning. A man who owns his actions owns his identity."

Enzo stood to signal the end of our conversation, and I followed suit. He walked towards me and extended his hand. "This is not the way I was hoping things would work out, but you have stated your company's case clearly and unequivocally. I wish you the best going forward from here and safe travels back to your home. Anna has arranged for a driver who is waiting outside to return you to the airport. Arrivederci, my friend."

And with that, I was left standing alone in the conference room, utterly defeated and crushed by what I knew to be the inevitable end of my life as I knew it.

shift

*Touchstones are simple but
evocative and powerful words,
ideas, thoughts, objects,
rituals and practices that
reconnect you to your
inspiration and intentions
so you aren't easily derailed
from your purpose.*

–Annabel Melnyk

chapter fifteen

I collected my luggage from Anna at the reception desk and was met by my driver just outside the grand entrance. "Are you ready to return to Malpensa International, Signore Jericho?" he asked politely.

"More than you'll ever know," I managed to respond.

"Buono," he replied. "Shall we make any stops en route possibly? For a meal or for provisions for your flight back home?"

"That's kind of you to offer, but I suddenly have no appetite. Directly to the airport is what I need most right now, but thank you."

"Very well, Signore. Directly to the airport, it will be."

We rode in silence for the better part of an hour until the driver pulled into a lane inside the airport designated for professional transport. I gathered my belongings and emptied my pocket of all the remaining euros I had without bothering to count the total. Whether generous or stingy, I would never know as he graciously accepted my tip and deposited it in his front pocket without counting it.

"Best of luck, Signore, with your return home."

"Grazie, best of luck to you as well."

Check-in, baggage drop, security, customs, and every other global entryway I passed through moved smoothly and uneventful. Forty-five minutes after arriving at the airport, I was already sitting at my departure gate, passing the remaining hour until boarding time by catching up on email and checking the national news to see what had happened since I'd left home.

"Tensions in the Middle East Rise."

"Homes in the Metroplex Surge in Value."

"Chinese Investors Seek to Acquire More US-based companies."

Geez, it's like I never left. These are the same headlines that were up when I left town. Guess it's good to know I didn't miss much. In a moment of dark humor, I couldn't resist crafting a few personal headlines for my own dark future:

"Sales Rep Singlehandedly Brings Down Major Supply Company."

"Misprint Brings Catastrophic Failure—One Man to Blame."

"Epic Failure Brings David Jericho to His Knees."

I stopped before my musings got the better of me, and I decided to stretch my legs and grab a carry-on meal for later rather than risk whatever was being offered on board. By the time I returned to the gate, they were calling for Boarding Group #7 to board. No Business Class upgrade for this flight. I would be jammed in a coach seat for 13 hours, but at least, it was a direct flight home. Within 30 minutes, the plane was taxiing towards the runway, and we were cleared for take-off.

Settling in for the long flight, I began to replay the unbelievable set of circumstances that had brought me to this point. I wouldn't have believed the story if it hadn't happened to me. I mean, what were the chances of all this happening *to one guy, in just over one day, all because of one incorrectly sent email.* Talk about a perfect storm…of failure. In little more than 24 hours, I had lost the account, almost assuredly lost my job, misrepresented my company, and grossly disappointed our most promising potential client. "When you go down, Jericho, you go big."

As I considered the final outcome of the day, I honestly didn't know what ultimately bothered me the most—letting so many at my home company down or disappointing what I had quickly come to regard as a sage, older gentleman, and his team. After all, I reasoned, winning the account and possibly saving the company was a longshot at best; though more likely a wasted act of desperation. In the end, it was the unexpected friendship and admiration I had come to feel for Saggio-turned-Enzo that was harder for me to accept.

I began replaying our time together, moment by moment, starting with our first meeting. From the very beginning, he had seen a glimmer of hope in me and had given myself every

shift

opportunity in the world to try and help me, both personally and professionally. Saggio had kindly and respectfully shared many of the guiding principles that had helped him succeed throughout his own life—a life I had foolishly thought to be no more than demanding than driving others to *their* places of importance.

And again, in the conference room, both Enzo and his team had tried and tried unsuccessfully to encourage me to stand behind the erroneously sent proposal—*my proposal*—and yet I had chosen to stand behind the excuse of company loyalty, blaming my unwillingness to present my original proposal on company management—a force I could not or would not challenge.

Still, as hopeless as my future undoubtedly appeared, there was something to all of Saggio's words that I just couldn't move past. What was it he said about a shift—all that went into making a successful shift? I began wracking my brain, pushing aside the dismal state of my career for the moment, to remember the words of hope and encouragement and challenge Saggio had shared throughout our travels.

I grabbed the cocktail napkin beneath my plastic cup and the pen from my coat pocket and began writing as fast as I possibly could. One thought led to another and then another; one memory triggered another as I replayed our journey and the principles Saggio had so subtly shared with me. Before I knew it, both sides of the napkin were covered in hastily written phrases and keywords, some underlined, some circled, some scratched through.

The rhythm of my writing was interrupted by a passing flight attendant. "Sir, would you like a small notepad? Or possibly another napkin?" she asked.

I smiled and remembered I had grabbed a couple of sheets of the exquisite hotel stationary as a memento of my first stay at a five-star hotel in Italy. "No thanks. I'm good." As the flight attendant left my aisle, I returned to my transcribing, fearful I would forget some significant detail or story from Saggio's lessons.

Eventually, my thoughts slowed and my hand began to cramp from the tight grip I had on my pen. I hadn't even realized the intensity of my note taking until I tried to unpeel my fingers from the barrel of the pen. "Guess I got a little inspired," I said to the lady seated beside me as she watched me work to restore the blood flow to my fingers.

When I felt as if I had thoroughly replayed every last incident, every last story, every last bit of relatable wisdom from Saggio, I sat back to review my notes. Within minutes, I realized a pattern was developing—every time Saggio would shift gears in his Ferrari, he would seem to have some words of wisdom for me that related to a change or transition that happened in someone's life, and somehow it applied to me. I realized he was talking about a SHIFT. A shift in the way I think about life. A shift in how I treat people. A shift in how I see my career.

Then it occurred to me it is much more than that. It is a systematic way about how to move from *where you are* to *where you want to go* in life smoothly and effectively.

shift

And then, the wisdom of Saggio all fell into place.

Suddenly, the keywords, the ones I had circled and elaborated the most upon, clearly stood out to me. "I get it!," I said out loud. "SHIFT! A SHIFT! I see it now—everything Saggio was telling was about how to SHIFT! The S, the H, the I, F, T— every letter stands for what's behind navigating a successful life!" It had been right there in plain sight the whole time! I had just read a book that Jenny had given me at Christmas, 'The Power of Moments," by Chip and Dan Heath. And I remembered one of the best lines in the book that had stuck with me— "You can change anyone's mind—if you help them trip over the truth." That's what I had been doing—*the whole time I was with Saggio...er, Enzo!* I was literally "tripping over the truths" that Saggio kept sharing with me. That's why he kept circling back to the importance of understanding all that is involved in making a worthwhile shift!

I was so pumped by my realization of Saggio's hidden-in-plain-sight principles and proofs; I had to work back through all I had written so that I could fully appreciate my new-found wisdom. I flipped to a clean sheet of paper and began summarizing as best I could my understanding of what went into a successful shift. I wanted to remember this moment and these words. "This counsel from Saggio—all that he showed me, all that he told me, all that he did to prepare and empower me—these words will be my manifesto moving forward," I said quietly to myself.

And then I wrote across the top in large capital letters: THE MANIFESTO OF DAVID JERICHO. From there, I read and re-read my notes, occasionally stopping to transfer a key phrase or idea to my newly named manifesto. When I was done, I sat back in my chair to take it all in:

THE MANIFESTO OF DAVID JERICHO

Seek Advice

→ WHEN CONFRONTED WITH SITUATIONS OUTSIDE OF MY AREAS OF DIRECT KNOWLEDGE, I WILL <u>SEEK OUT</u> PEOPLE AND RESOURCES THAT WILL OFFER ME INSIGHT, WISDOM, AND DIRECTION. IN RETURN, I WILL <u>BE A SOURCE</u> OF INSIGHT, WISDOM, AND DIRECTION <u>FOR OTHERS</u>.

Honor my Past

→ I HONOR WHAT HAS SHAPED ME INTO THE PERSON THAT I AM. I WILL USE MY PAST CHALLENGES AND SUCCESSES AS A SPRINGBOARD TO MY FUTURE. I WILL <u>REPLACE</u> THE PHRASE "I SHOULD HAVE", WITH "<u>NEXT TIME I WILL</u>."

Investigate the Options

→ THERE ARE VARIOUS ROADS TO SUCCESS. I WILL <u>BE OPEN</u> TO TAKING THE BETTER ROAD, THOUGH IT MAY NOT ALWAYS BE THE <u>EASY</u> OR THE MOST OBVIOUS. NEITHER FEAR NOR PRIDE WILL STOP ME OR LIMIT MY OPTIONS.

Focus on my Purpose

→ I WILL <u>SEEK</u> TO FIND AND FOLLOW MY LIFE'S PURPOSE. I WILL EMBRACE EVERYTHING THAT'S PURPOSEFUL AND DISCARD EVERYTHING THAT ISN'T. I WILL USE MY PURPOSE TO <u>INSPIRE OTHERS</u>.

Take Ownership

→ I ALONE AM RESPONSIBLE FOR MY ACTIONS. I <u>WILL NOT BLAME</u> OTHERS. I AM THE OWNER OF MY CHOICES. THE BUCK STOPS WITH ME.

shift

This is what Saggio had been telling me this all along, literally from the moment we met. He was intentionally showing me how to take the shifts in life and learn from them and grow from them and how to best benefit from the opportunities they *always* present.

This was a complete transformation for me—an incredibly new way of approaching life and all its messy and unexpected detours. And it came at a time I had just moments earlier considered being at the low point of my life. Instead, from my seat some 30,000 feet above the Atlantic Ocean, I was filled with gratitude for finally understanding the wise counsel and instruction of an Italian gentleman I initially thought to be nothing more than my personal chauffeur. What a sobering realization—to think I had discounted Saggio at first, going so far as to presume he had few aspirations beyond driving others around.

Now, I was filled with gratitude over what I had learned and even experienced on this trip.

Now, I knew the tools I needed to weather this storm and the steps to take to thrive in the days ahead.

Now, I was gratified that my ideas were considered worthy by others—significant others, well outside the walls of my office.

Now, I was ready to shift.

shift

It is never too late

to be what you

might have been.

– George Eliot

chapter sixteen

As expected, the week after my return to the office was a rough one…followed by *several* rough weeks. It was no surprise to me that we didn't win the Enzo account and I had done my best to lower expectations with Barry so that the news wasn't a complete shock. I don't think he ever really considered it a strong possibility—the one-in-a-million chance to save our jobs, if not the entire company—but his disappointment could be heard throughout the entire office anyway. Always one to overreact and leave no blame left unplaced; he let it be known to all within earshot that if he'd been able to make the trip, he was certain the account would have been ours.

Poor guy. I had actually come to feel sorry for him since my return from Italy. Full of bluster and an overly active sense of bravado, his final outrage was met with little more than shrugged shoulders and eye rolls by all of us 'minor players.' He had his moment, and we moved on.

shift

Though not for very long.

The following week, a company-wide email informed every one of us, as B + L employees, that the takeover by Xi Chang, Ltd. was in the final stages of completion and that HR would be scheduling meetings with every employee to notify us whether or not we had a job going forward.

As part of the management team, I was one of the first to be notified. My HR rep broke the news as kindly as possible, but gracious thank-yous for my many years of service aside, the result was the same: I was out of a job. There was a silver lining; however, to my termination—a six-month severance and benefits package that made the whole experience not just palpable, but downright promising.

I had money and insurance to carry us through for the short-term. I had the wisdom and insight of a tremendously accomplished older gentleman in my back pocket. And I was primed to put everything I'd learned from him into practice.

It was a perfect storm of opportunity…the opportunity to make the most significant SHIFT of my life.

On Day One of my new life, I set up shop in our spare bedroom. It had always been a catch-all for short-lived hobbies and out-of-season clothes for the girls but going forward; it was the original home of Jericho Enterprises. And it suited me perfectly in the early days—humble surroundings, humbled guy.

I was so anxious to start seeing how I could apply Saggio's SHIFT principles to my life; I woke up on my own at 5:30 a.m. I knew it was useless to try and go back to sleep, so I made some coffee and got to work. Until 10:00 p.m.

As I did the next day too.

And the next.

And the next.

I literally could not turn my brain off as one new idea or one new concept came into focus right after another. Jenny kept me fed and caffeinated with regular sandwich and coffee refills. She even mentioned she hadn't seen me this excited about work since before graduation. I told her I was onto something—and that 'something' was the SHIFT of a lifetime for me and us.

With Saggio's words and wisdom as the basis of my manifesto, I honestly was more excited and hopeful about my future than I had been since graduating college. I even enlarged my hand-written manifesto and had it printed poster size and kept it in front of me as a constant reminder of my endgame.

I started at the beginning—with the 'S' and the challenge to seek advice—and worked my way through the challenge of each letter. I made a list after list of possible contacts, both close friends and professional contacts. The only criteria were that they needed to have succeeded on their own or have some vital skill set I did not have or someone I wanted to learn from. I did not seek advice from casual acquaintances or just from family, who though they love me, do not have what I need to start and run a business. I wanted the advice and counsel of men and women who had forged their own path and overcome their own set of career hurdles and setbacks. I wanted to talk with others who have done what I was trying to do. I considered men and women who had expertise in areas where I had none. I selected a business coach who became a great teacher and sounding board. And there were others. Many eventually came to form my personal board of advisors, providing counsel and direction as I needed. Saggio showed me that I cannot know everything and that I can learn from others, i.e., in essence, I can borrow their knowledge.

My college buddies were among my first contacts as I knew they could be trusted to shoot straight with me about all they'd been through to get to where they were today. There were no pretenses in our group; we wouldn't have stood for it. After all, we had lived together in a house that was literally falling around us for four years.

I also scheduled few appointments with Jenny as a way of involving her in the early days of the process. I needed her buy-in, and I wanted to prove to her that I valued her support and input. I also wanted to make it clear that she was an integral part of this new adventure. We laughed and talked and dreamed about the business, the girls, our future, and *us*. Jenny had ideas and suggestions I would never have thought of on my own and fast became my most-valued sounding board. The connection we made in the early days of the company gave our marriage a second wind as it was the first time I had ever really intentionally sought and valued her perspective on business concerns.

Saggio, of course, became a principal advisor who I turned to many times in the early days, and still do to this day, seeking his input about processes and plans, theories and applications. I asked about broad-reaching marketing plans versus finely tuned niche appeals. I asked, and I asked, and I asked. And then he shared the most critical business concept I'd ever heard. He said, "David, never forget—you are not simply creating a product to be consumed. You are *serving* people by means of your products and services. Whatever it is you are selling your customers, their patronage is a privilege." I've never forgotten the insight this shift in perspective gave me. We still visit frequently, but now more so about matters well beyond business.

After having worked through seeking the advice of what came to be my advisory committee, I then took a small retreat to the Texas Hill Country. It was a time to be alone and reflect on my career and to pay honor to my past, both professionally and relationally. I was brutally honest with myself as I worked through how I had gotten to where I was at this point in my life. I took stock of the wise and the not-so-wise career decisions I'd made, as well as the paths I could have chosen. It took a lot of soul-searching to evaluate what I'd done right and where I'd found success, but it required even more strength to confront my failures and what they had cost me in terms of advancement and relationships. It was a turning point when I came to realize my greatest successes had come when I acted upon my passions and strengths. It was, even more, convicting to accept that my biggest failures had come when I acted against my better judgment or only to please others.

Historically at this juncture, I would have become paralyzed with regret and frustration, a reaction I easily defaulted to. But this time was different. This time I knew better. And this time, I had it within me to recommit to never going against what I knew to be the right thing to do. I was ready to move past former success and beyond my mistakes and go forward. This time was different because I was intentionally choosing not to regret my past, but to honor and learn from it.

It was clear I had a few solid options I should investigate regarding my career. The easy fix to my unemployment status was just to get another job, presumably another corporate job like the one I had just been released from. Believe me, the temptation was there, and it would have paid the bills. But it was Jenny, who was enjoying my new-found passion and energy and outlook on life, who urged me to stay on track. And she was right.

I honestly couldn't fathom signing on with another distributor, working for God knows who and bending to another company's culture. Sure, I needed insurance for my family but at what cost? I would find a way to provide for them without selling out.

Most of my peers from B + L jumped back into the corporate chaos and thought I was crazy for not grabbing a job while I was still fresh from the buyout. Like the old colleague I ran into at Starbucks who said, "You're going to regret not striking while the iron is hot, Jericho." I'll admit that his words made me doubt my plan, but only for a moment. I knew he meant well, and that I was undoubtedly choosing what many considered 'the hard road,' but I also knew it was the only path that would allow me to follow my passions. I had to take the chance. It was that or spend the rest of my life regretting it and wondering 'what if?'

Don't get me wrong—I'm not saying it was an easy journey—by no means. But it was the right one for me. These past five years have undoubtedly been the most rewarding of my entire professional life. And I thank God every day for the opportunity I have to run my own company. It has even allowed me to fulfill another promise I made to myself to give back. I now sit on the board of a non-profit that is helping to end childhood hunger in the poorest parts of Dallas. Our company has provided thousands of meals for kids and families who are struggling in our town.

Early on, I knew I was laying the foundation of something great. I had a team of trusted and successful advisors, I had confronted and resolved my past failures, and just as importantly, I was setting the stage for success and fulfillment—both of which had escaped me in my previous jobs. I came to appreciate and recognize and even celebrate the experiences and strengths I had gained in reaching this point because I now understood the perspective they gave me and how they had prepared me to thoroughly investigate all the opportunities before me *now*.

When I only had three months left from my severance, my challenge was to stay calm and *stay focused*. In the past, I had always been prone to exciting grand ideas about how I would run things if I were in charge. To be sure, I had the ideas; I just had no follow-through. I'd start out all fired up and ready to take action but would quickly get overwhelmed at the first hint of resistance or other difficulties. I knew laser-like focus would have to become second nature to me if I was to have any chance of making through the first years of running my own business.

I'd read the statistics and heard the war stories of guys losing everything they had, and I didn't want to join their ranks. I determined to be the exception, the example, even the inspiration for others to follow their passion.

As it turned out, having written out my manifesto on the plane ride back from Milan provided what I had been missing all along—a purpose about which I was passionate about and a purpose against which I could rely upon to make decisions and weigh options. Armed with my purpose, the process of strengthening my focus quickly was greatly simplified. When faced with the consideration of next steps to take or decisions to be made, I held the options up against the charge of my manifesto. If it is aligned, I accepted it; if not, I dismissed it and moved on. If I was unsure, I sought advice from my advisors.

That's not to say I didn't veer off course now and then, because I did *and still do*, but now I know how to correct it and get right back on track. Just the presence of a defined purpose with a few checkpoints along the way has relieved much of the fear I would have generally felt about starting my own company. My purpose gave me security and clarity, and focus wasn't so difficult anymore.

The final and most significant part of my shift came when I realized and accepted the fact that I had to take ownership for everything I'd done to this point in my life and everything I did going forward. Good or bad, prosperous or not, my decisions and their outcomes were *all mine*. This was, by far, the most painful, yet most beneficial lesson I learned from Enzo. Through his example and that of many others, he taught me what every great leader knows—in order to lead well and effectively; you must stand by your beliefs, act upon them to the best of your ability, and then accept complete responsibility for the outcome. There was no allowance for excuses or blame. With the title came the responsibility. End of discussion.

I chose not to be a victim of other peoples' choices but took ownership of my life, and that is how Jericho Enterprises came to be. Through lots of trial and error, lots of early missteps, and lots of reversing and resetting the path we were on. But I wouldn't change it for the world.

Not one day of praying for somebody—*anybody*—to take a chance on us.

Not one day of taking the fall for someone else's mistake.

Not one day of working through the weekend to far exceed a potential client's expectations to win the account.

None of it; because *all of it* has gotten us where we are today. I was fortunate enough to have someone share with me the principles I needed to make a shift—*a real shift*—that would forever change my life and that of my family's. And so now, I am paying it forward to you.

I paused realizing that I had been telling Tom my story for almost two hours.

"Hey, sorry. I didn't realize that I had been talking for so long. But you can see how passionate I am about this. I hope it doesn't take you nearly as long as it took me to make the shift of a lifetime."

Tom spoke for the first time. "No, Mr. Jericho. I am honored that you shared your story with me. I've gotta tell you that I recognize myself in it. I know that I am not that far into my career, but I relate to everything you've said. I want to have more than an ordinary career too. I have a mission but haven't had the courage to pursue it. So, thank you!"

I stood up and shook Tom's hand, "You're welcome, Tom. If I can ever be of assistance to you on your journey, please don't hesitate to call."

"And now, I should probably drive you back to the office before ol' Barry comes after both of us!" We both laughed thinking about Barry pacing back and forth in his office.

Tom and I left the conference room and took the elevator down to the garage level. On the ride down, I could tell Tom was lost in thought, but I also thought I caught a glimpse of hopefulness in his face too. When we reached the garage level, the doors opened, and we stood facing the only car left in the parking garage, a 1996 Ferrari F355 Spider.

"This is your car?!" Tom's statement came out as a part question and part astonishment.

"Yes. Every time I drive this car, it reminds me of where it all started, with the advice I got from a wise Italian driver."

"Do you want to drive it?" I asked before tossing him the keys.

He didn't hesitate for a second. "Absolutely"!

I took my place beside him in the passenger's seat while Tom started the car. The engine made the dulcet growl well-taken care of Ferraris are known for.

"Take a left onto 5th street. You'll know where to go from there," I told him.

Tom chuckled. "You're right. I think I may understand how to get where I want to go. Thank you, Mr. Jericho."

shift

*You're only one shift
away from the life
you want.*

– John Hinkle

epilogue

SHIFT PRINCIPLES DEFINED

That is the purpose of this book and our company—to help *you* learn the steps and the skills *to shift* in the best possible way. This book illustrates the five principles that anyone who is considering (or is already in the midst of) a significant career or personal transition can use to help guide their future. While each of the principles are distinct, they don't necessarily need to be followed in order. In fact, it is highly likely you will find some of the learnings from one principle can be applied to and enhance your understanding of the other principles.

When you adopt the SHIFT Principles described in this book and use them as tools to approach and navigate the challenges of change, you will be better equipped in all areas of your life because *change is life.*

SEEK ADVICE - Seeking advice is the single-most critical action we can take during times of transition. But seeking advice requires a lot from us. It requires humility and the willingness to acknowledge that we can't truly make it on our own. Nobody can and nobody does. There are always people in the background that we rely upon. Humility helps us admit we are strongest when we rely on the strength of others.

Seeking Advice requires us to be vulnerable and to risk exposing our shortcomings and weaknesses and fears to others. It means being receptive to accepting input from others and their assessment of where we stand and the options before us. It does not mean that we should follow every advice given us, but just receive it with an open mind for consideration. And finally, seeking advice requires trust—trust in selecting trustworthy sources and trust in ourselves to act upon the good advice received.

GOOD advice from good sources is essential to moving forward in the change moments of life. But how do you go about getting good advice? Most of us have many people in our life who are more than happy to offer their opinions, but it can be challenging to sort out the good advice from bad advice. And it can be equally hard to separate the good, well-meaning advisors from the inadequate ones?

In our practice of working with men and women who are trying to manage a substantial career change, we hear a lot of stories of discouragement and career setbacks all because they accepted well-meaning advice from inadequate advisors.

But it doesn't have to be that way.

In our SHIFT Principles courses, workshops, and coaching, we help clients set up their own Board of Advisors. We show you the four types of advisors you need for support and how they will serve you.

Honor the Past - Honoring the past is not about idolizing the past. It is about the acknowledgment of what shaped you and the perspective it provides going forward. Behind every life or career change is a history of setbacks and achievements, wins and losses, regrets and gratitude. In SHIFT, our protagonist David Jericho, experiences all of these. His transitional moment occurs when he realizes what a significant role his past has played into where he is today *and* a valuable context for how he can shape his future.

It works the same for each of us. Each of our past experiences are a piece of the fabric that makes up a sail—a sail that can push us forward or can hold us back.

In working through the SHIFT Principles, we help you explore the key milestones in your life and career that are sometimes difficult to explore, but that can oftentimes hold the key for making a successful shift. Some of these milestones include:

a. **Losses and Gains** – Identifying where in your career or life you have been most successful as well as where you have you struggled the most;

b. **Influencers and Dissuaders** - Determining who or what has had the greatest impact on your life and career and who or what has kept you from moving forward;

c. **Packing and Unpacking** - Deciding what to take with you on your next step and what to leave behind;

INVESTIGATE THE OPTIONS – It's an old saying, but one that bears repeating when discussing the value in investigating our options: *"We can't predict the future, but we can shape it."*

The road ahead is never fixed, regardless of what we may think or what others tell us. In fact, for better or for worse, everything in our life, both past and future, has been and *will always be* bound by our perspective, our attitude, our intentions, and our actions.

Every transition presents opportunities to freely investigate options and shape the future.

One of the most satisfying moments of our coaching and consulting work is when clients come to the realization of the freedom that comes with change. When they are able to uncover options previously considered unavailable and envision new and exciting goals, it is a game-changer!

In our workshops and coaching sessions, we help our clients to build a visual map, laying out goals and discovering potential paths to get there. We help them evaluate the options available to them and help to make certain that they are congruent with their goals and values, thereby crafting an exciting and promising life ahead.

FOCUS ON YOUR PURPOSE - During a career or life transition, it is natural to examine our values and reassess our life's purpose. In his book, *Start with Why,* author Simon Sineks states, "If you don't know why, you can't know how."[1] In SHIFT, we discuss how vision doesn't come easily, but that it's worth every bit of effort it takes to identify it.

For our team, and for most of our clients, we find that we are too nearsighted to completely fill in the lines of a distant vision. It's kind of like playing Pin the Tail on the Donkey at a kid's party—sometimes we've been spun around in such a way that we can't even determine which direction is right. In working with our clients, we help bring purpose and vision together in a clearer way.

TAKE OWNERSHIP - A turning point for our clients is when they identify and begin putting into action the SHIFT Principles necessary to chart a successful shift. To do so requires a big step--taking ownership and accepting the responsibility for their actions and attitude. It takes courage, determination, and faith, but it is the final step necessary in moving forward. More specifically this means having the courage to live with the decisions they have made, the determination not to give up when things get tough, and faith in both yourself and God.

This may be the hardest principle of all because this is where the *real* change happens. It is also where a lot of people get stuck. They may be able to acknowledge, accept, and

---

1   Simon Sinek, "Start with Why"- Penguin Group, 2009

organize around change, but become stuck when it's time to take ownership of the change and begin taking action.

Once a course of action is determined, we must own the decision, own the process, and own the results. In other words, it requires a 'the buck stops here' mindset. For our clients, we walk through seven concepts that are key to taking ownership, and like David Jericho, we help you create your own manifesto—*a written declaration of your intentions, motives, and commitments.*

We have created a workshop experience designed to assist participants with crafting an effective SHIFT plan along with other valuable resources. Visit www.SHIFTprinciples.com for more details.

our story

The SHIFT Principles Group is dedicated to helping people, organizations, and teams learn how to successfully manage change. Our core belief is that shift is unavoidable and the best way to handle the inevitable is through knowledge and perspective. Armed with these, change loses its power to control us.

Our purpose is to give every person and every company we serve the life-changing insights and tools necessary make a positive life change. We work with businesses, corporate leaders, churches, and individuals across the US. If you are interested in engaging The SHIFT Principles Group to work with your team or are interested in one-on-one coaching, Contact: John@SHIFTprinciples.com.

shift

*The most difficult thing is the
decision to act, the rest is
merely tenacity. The fears
are paper tigers. You can
do anything you decide to do.*

–Amelia Earhart

john's shift story

In 2010, after 25 years of climbing the corporate ladder and achieving success as a corporate leader, I began my own SHIFT journey. Much like our protagonist, David Jericho, my career seemed to have stalled.

I was dissatisfied.

Burned out.

And my career certainly didn't seem sustainable for another 20 years.

It was during this time, I was meeting with my C12 Group, a group of fellow corporate leaders who meet regularly to focus on studying the Bible and to share business and life experiences with one another—along the lines of 'iron sharpening iron' mindset. It was during this time I came to realize each of us in the group were frustrated and dissatisfied with many aspects of our corporate lives. After a lot of heartfelt and transparent discussion,

shift

it became apparent—all of us, whether formally or informally, were exploring career and life transitions. Unknowingly, we were *all* priming ourselves for a shift.

That led me to begin exploring the whole idea with my colleagues to better grasp what we were all considering. But before I jumped head-first into this major transition, I wanted to fully understand what the whole process looked like—the steps that would be necessary to take, the potential impact it could have on me, my family, and our lifestyle, the realistic sacrifices, and the hopeful end-game results.

I started talking with career advisors about the subject. I consulted psychologists who specialized in working with people undergoing significant life changes. I read story after story of men and women who had been through tremendous life changes—some of their own doing, some beyond their control. Before long, I began to notice a pattern: the ones who went beyond—*well beyond*—not just surviving their personal transitions, but excelling and charting new paths, new lifestyles, and *new and better lives,* consistently followed and practiced many of the same principles. I began making notes on one person and then another—why they took *that* next step, *who* helped them along the way, *where* they went from there, and so on. Time after time, whatever the specifics of their story, I found these people followed similar paths to overcoming their personal crises; they adjusted their course, drew from their experiences, and went on to consider their setback *the catalyst* for making a life-altering transition.

I was so encouraged and inspired by the consistency of my findings and the apparent relationship between achieving professional success and personal fulfillment and following these practices, I felt led to simplify, refine, *and share* my findings with others.

The results are the SHIFT Principles, a dynamic, challenging, yet proven and satisfying, step-by-step business practice focused on helping people make better career choices and better life transitions.

shift

I skate to where the
puck is going to be,
not where it has been.

– Wayne Gretzky

russell's shift story

I have not always shifted well. I have always been good
at investigating the options and figuring things out on my own.
That worked some of the time, or at least I thought it did. One
such event was while working within the business that my
father started, a commercial recording studio. While he operated
the studio business, I operated the manufacturing and design
divisions of the company. We were growing fast and the demand
for our services was out pacing our ability to complete the projects
at the speed I felt they needed to be done. An opportunity arose
that I felt would save the day and propel us to the next level. I
dove head first into a merger with another firm without seeking
the advise of anyone. That turned out to be a huge mistake that
took me many years to recover from.

I tend to be a person who says "yes" to requests and
projects and then work to figure out how to do it once the job is

shift

won. This has produced some wonderful relationships and has allowed me to expanded my skills to include: product design and manufacturing, leading a design agency, helping authors publish books, directing live stadium events, and filmmaking. This broad experience has the accumulated effect of "magically" putting me in the right place at the right time. In addition to SHIFT Principles, my current endeavor is a national television production that uses all the skills from my past in an amazing way. I never set out to write a book, produce a television show or make a feature film when I graduated college with a degree in finance, but here I am. I did not know it then, but I utilized the SHIFT principles as I took on this new adventure. I can tell you that these principles work, and while they do not guarantee success, they can place you in the best possible position for success.

acknowledgments

We would like to thank the following people for your insights, encouragement, and SHIFT stories that have had a profound impact on our work.

☐ Thank you to Cheryll Duffie for help bringing this story to life.

☐ Thank you to our friends who have shared their SHIFT stories and given so much encouragement. Joe Petersen, Dr. Paul Douthit, Dr. John Lee, Joe Ward, John Milam, Jan Lee, Geoff Mantooth, Kevin Freeman, Mike Carter, Jason DeLaPorte, Randy Draper and many more.

☐ Thanks to our growing SHIFT tribe who are spreading the word that anyone is only one shift away from achieving success.

☐ Finally, we give thanks for everything and all praise and glory to our Lord who desires for everyone to live with purpose.

shift

The journey of a thousand miles begins with one step.

– Lao Tzu

additional resources

Visit SHIFTprinciples.com, and explore:

Consulting: Highly trained SHIFT Principle advisors teach the SHIFT Principles in through group or individual consulting and training sessions. Our sessions are insightful, practical, engaging, and transformative.

Contact John@SHIFTprinciples.com to book a session for your group.

One-on-One Coaching: Our consultants are trained to help clients navigate career and life changes. To learn more about working with a SHIFT Principle Coach, contact, Coach@SHIFTprinciples.com.

Speaking Engagements: John Hinkle brings the SHIFT Principle concept to audiences around the US. If you want John to speak at your event, contact, booking@SHIFTprinciples.com.

SHIFT Course and Retreat: SHIFTprinciples.com.

shift

SHIFTprinciples.com

CPSIA information can be obtained
at www.ICGtesting.com
Printed in the USA
LVHW081158160820
663323LV00012B/283/J